Advance praise for *The Church Cracked Open*

"If you are looking at the landscape of the church and wondering, 'How'd we get here?' and what's next, I invite you to board Rev. Spellers's plane and take in the big picture with her. Take in the history, the theology, the pain, the beauty, and the hope that her view from thirty thousand feet offers. When she lands the plane, you'll realize—there's simply no better guide out there."

—Nadia Bolz-Weber, author

"Stephanie Spellers draws our attention to the unraveling of white Christianity in the face of contextual diversity and Jesus's cross. She invites her readers to stop negotiating with the past and to realize that love is not maintaining and protecting community but the very cracking open at the heart of community. This book continues the theology of James Cone and Kelly Brown Douglas and signals a cruciform direction."

—C. Andrew Doyle, IX Bishop, Episcopal Diocese of Texas

"In a moment when structures and patterns in the church's life are being deeply disrupted, this book is a loving, passionate invitation to repent, reimagine, and renew by rediscovering the church's identity in the triune God's healing of the world. Stephanie Spellers not only names hard truths but also and even more importantly offers hope and promise in Jesus's way of love."

—Dwight Zscheile, PhD,
VP of Innovation and Associate Professor
of Congregational Mission and Leadership,
Luther Seminary, St. Paul, Minnesota

THE
CHURCH
CRACKED
OPEN

THE CHURCH CRACKED OPEN

Disruption, Decline, and New Hope for Beloved Community

Stephanie Spellers

CHURCH
PUBLISHING
INCORPORATED

Unless otherwise noted, the Scripture quotations are from New Revised Standard
Version Bible, copyright © 1989 National Council of the Churches of Christ in the
United States of America. Used by permission. All rights reserved worldwide.

Scriptures quotations marked (KJV) are taken from the KING JAMES VERSION
(KJV): KING JAMES VERSION, public domain.

Church Publishing
19 East 34th Street
New York, NY 10016
www.churchpublishing.org

Cover design by Jennifer Kopec, 2Pug Design
Typeset by PerfecType, Nashville, Tennessee

Library of Congress Cataloging-in-Publication Data

Names: Spellers, Stephanie, author.
Title: The church cracked open : disruption, decline, and new hope for
  beloved community / Stephanie Spellers.
Identifiers: LCCN 2020046843 (print) | LCCN 2020046844 (ebook) | ISBN
  9781640654242 (paperback) | ISBN 9781640654259 (ebook)
Subjects: LCSH: Church. | Communities--Religious aspects--Christianity. |
  Episcopal Church. | Christian life. | Mary Magdalene, Saint.
Classification: LCC BV625 .S69 2021 (print) | LCC BV625 (ebook) | DDC
  260--dc23
LC record available at https://lccn.loc.gov/2020046843
LC ebook record available at https://lccn.loc.gov/2020046844

CONTENTS

On Being Cracked Open

It was Saturday, August 1, 2020. I know because my text log tells me so. That afternoon I wrote to a friend:

> God is breaking open this church and pouring us out—pouring out privilege, pouring out empire, pouring out racism and human arrogance—in order to remake us and use us to serve God's dream for the whole world. We are the broken jar. It hurts and it sucks . . . and I think it's a gift.

At that moment, we were six months into a global pandemic and economic collapse. It had been half a year since faith communities could fully and physically gather for prayer, worship, service, and fellowship. Many churches were flooded with need, just as donations began to dry up and our most reliable volunteers were locked away for fear of COVID-19. For six months people had been dying, sometimes more than a thousand a day in America, a disproportionate number of them Black, Latinx, and Indigenous people, whose lives the nation had long ago deemed "expendable."

We were two months from the horror of watching Minnesota police officer Derek Chauvin pin his knee on George Floyd's neck and squeeze the breath of life out of him. Two months into ongoing protest, truth-telling, reading groups, and deep grief for people of every race, but especially for my Black, Indigenous, Latinx, and Asian siblings. Two months shouting to God: "How long, Lord? Will you forget us forever? Must we have sorrow in our hearts all the day? How long shall our enemy be exalted over us?" (Psalm 13).

In the scope of human life, two months or even six months isn't that long. By the time you read these words, it may be a year or two (or ten) since these cataclysmic events. Other disasters might have eclipsed them entirely. I do not know. What I do know is that as this particular season wore on, something felt different. Others described the shift, too. Here is what we noticed:

First, loss and uncertainty were nothing new. America* and civic institutions and churches that once rested comfortably at her center had actually suffered disruption, decline, and displacement for decades before 2020.

Second, this was a new phase, a steeper drop, a more profound disruption and displacement. For more than a generation, people had been speaking of the churches' need to detach from our buildings, but now we were literally unable to congregate inside our sanctuaries in any significant numbers. Churches that once balked at a screen in the sanctuary were suddenly reconstructing church in cyberspace. People who had never before used words like "White supremacy" (more on this term and others later) were recognizing them as essential to understanding American identity and dominant American Christian culture.

Experts, scholars, and preachers agreed that this overall moment in American life was unlike anything most of us had previously faced. Leaders like Andy Crouch, Kurt Keilhacker, and Dave Blanchard explained that past experiences of disruption could be likened to a winter storm or maybe even a blizzard, but we were now in something like an extended winter season, maybe even an ice age.[1] The usual

---

*I ask your forbearance in advance, because I will be using "America/n" chiefly to speak of the United States of America, the focus of my research and reflection. Even as I do so, I'm aware that America is "a continent, not a country," as Guillermo Gómez-Peña observed in his landmark 1985 essay, "The Multicultural Paradigm: An Open Letter to the National Art Community."

institutional patterns and practices would not apply. It was time to act like a start-up.

Others compared the experience to wandering in the wilderness. Together with my wise colleague Dwight Zscheile, a professor of leadership and innovation at Luther Seminary, I hosted a summertime web series and podcast called "Wilderness Time" (find it at www .wildernesstime.org). For six weeks, we gathered practitioners, students, and thought leaders to explore life on the edge with God. Our trusty navigational devices would not work here, so we'd better learn to trust God to provide direction and sustenance, as the Israelites learned the hard way during their forty-year wilderness sojourn. Like our forebears, we would have to embrace uncertainty and loss, humbly recenter our lives with the margins, and fundamentally redefine what is holy, what is worship, and what makes a follower of Jesus.

Choose your metaphor: earthquake, blizzard, wilderness. This territory was unknown, and we weren't likely to find our way any time soon. There was no denying the truth: we needed God desperately.

The Woman Who Broke the Alabaster Jar

Casting about, searching for God's leading, my eye kept landing on one biblical image: a brazen woman with an alabaster jar full of costly, scented nard in her hands. The story shows up in all four gospels, but God kept drawing me to Mark's simple, action-packed account: "While [Jesus] was at Bethany in the house of Simon the leper, as he sat at the table, a woman came with an alabaster jar of very costly ointment of nard, and she broke open the jar and poured the ointment on his head" (Mark 14:3).

Like most commentators and preachers, I thought I knew the story: here was a woman who loved Jesus and sacrificed something precious in order to witness to that love. The disciples stormed and complained at her for wasting the oil *and* at Jesus for allowing her to approach in the first place. I've always been fond of Jesus in this story. Not only did he refuse to shun her, he got sassy with them and suggested they should be more like her. "Wherever the good news is proclaimed in the whole world, what she has done will be told in remembrance of her" (Mark 14:9).

The more I dwelled with the story, the more shocking it appeared. Can you imagine the scandal, as she walks into a dinner gathering of men hosted by a Pharisee? This woman carries a precious, alabaster-tiled jar of perfumed oil worth a year's wages. She is the essence of disruption, hijacking their senses of sight, smell, taste, and decency.

Does she offer the jar to the host or to Jesus? Maybe pour some nard into her hand and anoint Jesus? No, she breaks the alabaster jar. In a culture where women are seen but not heard and have so little public agency, she walks in unannounced and uninvited and breaks a jar. The crack and crash must have felt like lightning and thunder. That's OK. She has every intention of profoundly disrupting and decentering the proceedings. So she takes something precious and breaks it.

Then she pours the nard onto Jesus's head. It flows down and down, until it drenches his hair, beard, and shoulders. Our sister has no interest in a stingy drip-drip from the jar's small opening. She wants the healing nard to flow onto Jesus like rivers, like power, and there is only one way to get that kind of free flow. Crack it open.

Already, you can see why the Gospel of Luke assumes she's a sinner and later scholars painted her as a prostitute. What other type of woman would be wealthy enough to possess a jar of perfumed ointment and bold enough to walk into a room full of men? What kind of woman would initiate such a dramatic and sensuous (in the truest sense of the word) gesture? A woman of means. A woman with her own ideas. A woman to be reckoned with.

While everyone else freaks out, Jesus receives her offering and thanks her for preparing his body for death and burial, and he promises that her extravagant, prodigal tribute will be remembered and retold for generations to come.

What did Jesus notice and admire so much in her? He didn't see waste. He understood that she was literally giving up the best of what she had—the alabaster jar *and* the nard—because he mattered that much to her. He was the holy one, the center of her world, and she had reoriented her life around him as her focus.

He must have valued her ability to discern what's important. Some disciples obsessed over the container, but what good is an exquisite jar if the ointment it holds can't get out? Others were anxious about losing the expensive nard, but what good is life-giving ointment if you don't share it with people in their time of need? She broke the jar. She poured out the oil. God blesses her for it.

Finally, I imagine Jesus was relieved to see someone else finally operating outside the bounds of moderation, rationalism, and business-as-usual. He was about to be killed by the powers and principalities of this world. Unlike his other followers, she grasped the urgency of the moment, took a risk, and leapt to meet him in it.

I want to sit at the feet of this sister and tell her about today, about decline, pandemic, reckonings, loss, and disruption. I want to confide in her: "So much has cracked open. *We* have been cracked open. We don't know how to embrace the disruption, make the sacrifice, stop worshiping the beauty of the jar, and instead break it open so the healing substance inside can work its way into a world that so desperately needs it. We're tempted to scramble around and gather the pieces and reassemble the jar and scoop up the lost oil. And we're really terrified we might *be* the jar, broken open by God, for love of the world. Maybe that's what God wants, but it's not what most American church folks signed on for."

How might she respond? In my prayer, I hear her speaking these wise words, calming the storm even as she stirs the waters.

You and your church, you are holding a beautiful jar. You are used to grasping it with both hands, tilting and pouring the contents with moderation through the carefully crafted spout. Someday, you will have to break it open so the contents flow free, or God will do it for you.

You and your church, you think loving a thing means protecting and maintaining it exactly as it was handed to you. Someday,

you will understand what it means to love something enough to
let it crack apart and just sit with the pieces, notice what needs
to be removed for good, and then faithfully piece together what
matters most to make something more whole, something more
like what God intended all along. Someday, you will lose your
life and gain real life.

Oh child, this could be one of those times.

It's Our Time

What if we are indeed at that point where the most faithful act is to
accept the cracked reality of the things we loved most? Maybe you are
called to be the one to break it open. Perhaps you and your church are
the thing being *broken*, and your life, identity, and understanding of
reality are being poured out, all so that God's love might become the
true center of your life.

If any of that is true, we're going to need some help and we're
going to need each other.

That's where this book comes in. I've spent nearly thirty years
studying religion and society, covering religion as a newspaper jour-
nalist, developing and editing books for a church publishing house,
and serving as an ordained priest at the congregational, diocesan, and
now denominational levels. My greatest joy through it all has been
listening to people and discovering the connections and movements
of God's Spirit in the spaces between us. That's what I've tried to
present in this book: collected wisdom, distilled by one whose heart
is full of love and who is certain we stand at a historic crossroads.
Be warned, this book attempts to share hard stories and challenging
questions with tenderness and hope. I'm sure I've failed at times, but
I trust nothing separates us from God's amazing grace, even when
we've been utterly, irrevocably cracked open.

Where do we even begin such a journey? I suggest we get
grounded in this present moment, and that is the task of chapter
1, "The Reality of Disruption and Decline." The contemporary

experience of being decentered, disrupted, and displaced is nothing new for Christianity. As America has grown more multicultural and secular, the so-called "Euro-tribal" *churches* (more on this concept in the next chapter) have fallen to the margins. While that loss of privilege could inspire fear and handwringing, it could also prime us for a dramatic reorientation. Decades of disruption and decline— culminating in the crises of pandemic, economic collapse, and racial reckoning—might be the shove we need to recenter away from empire and onto God and God's dream.

In chapter 2, "New Hope for Beloved Community," we together imagine this better world, one where human beings release our grip on safety and prosperity, sacrifice for the sake of each other's flourishing, share one another's burdens, and live more like children made in the image of our unselfishly, extravagantly loving God. Think of this chapter as planting your feet, breathing deeply, and getting rooted in the hope for beloved community that Jesus and generations of theologians and prophets hold to this day. Let it be the bright star by which you set your course during the trek that follows.

So chapter 1 maps the overall picture of where we are, and chapter 2 points with initial hope to where we long ultimately to go. After that, you get the "come-to-Jesus" chapters, where we admit just how far America and her dominant Christian communities have wandered from God's dream.

Chapter 3, "The Origins of the Nightmare," explores the original sin of self-centeredness, or more precisely what I call "*self-centrism*," that is, organizing the world so that it rotates around you or your group. We will see how this selfish orientation has metastasized into empire, oppression, and White domination, and how these forces have shaped and contorted America.

In chapter 4, "The Church of Empire," I narrow the scope to examine my own Episcopal Church, that peculiar child of British Empire and American exceptionalism. Because of our unique history and privilege, we have often functioned as faithful chaplain to empire, upholding a tasteful banner to cover the sins of genocide, slavery, greed, segregation, and oppression. Every faith community has a story of choosing idols, ego, and sin over God. This is my church's.

Thanks be to God, these failures are neither the whole story nor the end of it. In chapter 5, "Shards of Light," we gather up stories of resistance, those holy moments when the Spirit has moved Episcopalians from self-centrism and privilege to embrace decentering and sacrifice, and to recenter with the persecuted and rejected. If a church like this one can reckon and be converted, there's hope for everyone.

Chapter 6, "Lose Your Life—Kenosis," looks more deeply still at what it takes to allow our hearts and structures to crack open in deep love for God and one another. In particular, we will explore the power of *kenosis*, the dramatic and voluntary pattern of release, non-clinging, and self-giving that marks Jesus's whole life. As his followers, we do not seek primarily to sustain the institutions we've built or the jars we've fashioned. Like the wise woman with the alabaster jar, we seek to triumph over fear and muster the courage to break the jar . . . or let God break and disrupt us.

After the cracking and decentering, do we race back to the center? Do we reassemble the pieces so they resemble the precious original? Or do we choose solidarity and recenter ourselves with Jesus, who so clearly cast his lot with the most vulnerable peoples? That's the topic of chapter 7, "Gain Your Life—Solidarity," which invites Christian communities once identified with the powers of empire and establishment to walk humbly with the oppressed, not only to relieve the suffering of the other, but because salvation and holiness await us all at the margins of empire.

Jesus gave us this dream. He also laid out a path for those who seek to follow him, release our grip on privilege, recenter on God, and live as beloved community. In the final chapter, "Walk in Love—Discipleship," I invite you to adapt the Way of Love, a rule of life Episcopalians and our friends use to walk together in the pattern of Jesus. I've tried to discern practical steps individuals, congregations, and ultimately a whole church can take to break from empire and self-centrism and reorient our lives around God, who is love. It's the only way I know that the oppressed and the oppressor can together experience freedom and abundant life.

I hope this book inspires more than deeper reflection. My fervent prayer is that you will examine your life and the life of your church, and the systems and assumptions that shape both. I hope you will become less anxious about how you and your community are cracking open, and more curious about how God might remake you as a true community of love. To help with that project, I have provided "*The Church Cracked Open*: Reflection & Action Guide" at www.church crackedopen.org (also available at the publisher's site, www.church publishing.org/churchcrackedopen). This free online tool includes even more original sources, reflection questions, and resources for further action. At various points throughout the book, I'll call out opportunities to use the guide to go deeper.

For now, our wise sister is reaching out, one hand filled with pieces of broken alabaster, the other hand open and gesturing to us. She says it's time to begin.

1

The Reality of Disruption
and Decline

There is nothing more tragic than to sleep through a revolution.
—Martin Luther King Jr.[1]

For some time now, church leaders have sat around tables and strategized, wringing our hands and sometimes engaging in wishful thinking about the ongoing systemic decline that has become a fact of life for *dominant American Christianity*. (Throughout the book, I will use this term to refer to the broad community of majority White, mainline Protestant and evangelical churches.) Global pandemic, the fear of economic collapse, and a massive racial comeuppance have added an extra degree of urgency and anxiety to those conversations. We sense and sometimes whisper the truth: dominant American Christianity has been displaced, pushed out of our buildings, away from our moorings, and out of the center . . . if there's any center left at all.

Protestant mainline churches have experienced systemic decline and displacement since the 1960s[2], and that trend has expanded over the last twenty years to engulf the United States' religious sector as a whole. It's worth noting that Christianity has blossomed at the very same time in Africa, Asia, and South America, as well as in Eastern Europe, China, and the Middle East. The most dynamic churches in the United States and the West are often comprised of people from these countries of origin.[3]

Back at home, across dominant American culture, entire generations are rejecting faith. Some are angry and associate Christianity with words like "hypocrite," "judgmental," and "anti-homosexual,"[4] but an alarming number of younger people simply do not know or care much about religious institutions at all.[5] If they notice us, they may see self-obsessed institutions bent on self-propagation. They may hear us promoting our churches as God's house. Since they've already met God outside, church isn't worth the extra hassle.

So if your church welcomes fewer people on a Sunday, and those who come tend to be less engaged all around, it's not going to change because the priest ups her preaching game, the musician brings in a drum, and you maintain a steady flow of online worship. The ground has shifted. The break is real.

I don't rejoice at this reality. The fact is, something fundamental about the American Christian story has been waiting to crack, like land stretched across a fault line. God knows, there have been plenty of tremors. Now it's a full-on break.

Religious commentator Phyllis Tickle pointed to this time as one of those periodic awakenings or "rummage sales" that Christianity holds every five hundred years or so, when it purges what's no longer useful and reforms itself for the age to come. In her final years, she promised we were entering "the Age of the Spirit," when our obsession with order and control would backfire, and we'd be forced to rely on the wily ways of the Holy Spirit. "Our jaws should drop open in amazement," she remarked at an Emerging Church conference in Memphis back in 2013 (I was sitting in the pews scribbling furiously).

"I think we're seeing a shift in Christianity as dramatic as that first Pentecost wildfire."

Our elder sister was more right than even she knew. Who could have predicted so much would crack, crack, and finally break open all at once? Now that it's happening, what do we do? We will address that last question in the chapters that follow. For now, I'd like to survey the disrupted cultural and social landscape all around.

The Great Unraveling

Alan Roxburgh is an excellent guide for starting our exploration. In his book *Joining God, Remaking Church, Changing the World*, he explores the story of a group of church families he calls the "Euro-tribal churches." These faith communities trace to the migration of peoples from England, Scotland, Ireland, and Northern Europe following the Reformations of the fifteenth and sixteenth centuries and the spread of colonial empires.[6] On this family tree, Episcopalians and Congregationalists trace to England, along with Baptists and Methodists (themselves an offshoot of Anglicanism). Presbyterians hail from Scotland. Lutherans carry Germany and Scandinavia in their DNA. Mennonites point back to the Netherlands and Germany.

Although they cast a global net now, these mostly White denominational families still identify with the cultural tendencies of their forebears. In many of these churches, including my own Episcopal Church, it's difficult to differentiate between what is holy and essential and what is actually racial, cultural, class preference. White identity and dominant American Christianity have been poured and blended into the same jar, and together they serve the purposes of empire.[7]

What does this familiar but loaded term mean? *Empire* is one country exercising power over another country, through colonial settlement but also through military domination, political sovereignty, or indirect means of control.[8] For example, the Roman and British empires extended into distant lands and relied on local assemblies and governors who recognized the sovereignty (or the rule) of Rome or England. American empire, on the other hand, has wielded control through military might and indirect mechanisms like economy and culture. Sociologist George Ritzer calls it the McDonaldization of the globe.

Colonialism can be understood almost as a subset of empire. The Oxford English Dictionary defines *colonialism* as "the policy or practice of acquiring full or partial political control over another country, occupying it with settlers, and exploiting it economically."[9] So, for instance, the British colonized by sending settlers who removed the original occupants, permanently occupied their lands, harnessed resources in the colony for the sake of the settlers and the imperial ruler, and otherwise established the empire's physical, political, and cultural power. The Euro-tribal churches were essential to that enterprise (we will visit this story in far greater detail in chapters 3 and 4).

Northern European cultural groups controlled much of American Christian life, even though they were not the only Christians here. In the 1700s and 1800s, Black people made up anywhere from one-sixth to one-third of the population of most colonies and states. Later, southern Europeans from Italy and Greece and their eastern European cousins brought an array of new smells, tastes, skin tones, and ways of being to America.

Faced with these non-dominant groups, the Euro-tribal churches had a choice: venture out, get to know the margins and newcomers, and create more culturally malleable Christian communities; or serve primarily as assimilating institutions that guide outsiders into subservient relationship to the White center.

At the risk of sweeping generalization, the Methodists and Baptists were more willing to invest energy and resources in the missionary venture, embracing outdoor revivals and bold ministry with Whites and Blacks, rich and poor. On the other end of the continuum, to varying degrees, Episcopalians, Lutherans, Mennonites, and Presbyterians preferred to welcome new people into their existing cultural enclaves . . . if they welcomed outside groups at all.

The latter assimilation strategy was sure to break down over time; logic and numbers demanded it. Immigrants were arriving with their own faith traditions, many of them Roman Catholic or Orthodox Christians, in addition to non-Christian groups like Jews (already present but ballooning because of European persecution), Muslims, Buddhists, Hindus, and more. Immigration laws were once engineered to artificially stem the flow and favor European migration. That ended in 1965, when America stopped fighting reality and the Immigration and Naturalization Act formally opened the doors and for a time eliminated pro-Europe, pro-White quotas.

That same year Congress passed the Voting Rights Act and protected Black people's right to the ballot box. The 1960s also gave life to fulsome movements for liberation among women and Chicanos (Mexican Americans) that in turn fueled movements for gay liberation, disability rights, and so much more. A generation grew up with their voices raised to claim civil rights and self-determination, and to push back at social hierarchies and restrictions. In other words, they pushed against the White, heterosexual, able-bodied men who were the face and voice of dominant American Christianity. The battle lines for the culture wars were drawn.

Beneath all these cultural and identity developments ran an even more fundamental shift: people asserting their right to have no faith at all. Since 1990, people who claim no faith tradition (the "Nones") have grown exponentially as a share of the American religious landscape.

By the turn of the twenty-first century, digital advances pushed the pace of cultural change into hyperdrive. In our book *The Episcopal Way*, Eric Law and I attempted to chart the seismic shifts rocking church and society,[10] from the internet and social media to brain functioning, networking and emergent theory to flattened authority, globalization to secularism. We concluded our analysis by noting, "The America we now inhabit is every bit wilderness, moving faster, filled with emerging voices and cultures, playing out in the flesh and online, the local going global and the global suddenly at the front door."[11]

America's dominant Christian groups tried to adapt for this wilderness sojourn, but they didn't get far. Coming out of the 1970s, the ascendant evangelical and Pentecostal churches embraced music, language, and especially media that reflected the surrounding culture, but they doubled down on conservative gender and political identities. Now they are the loudest and most recognizable voice of Christianity in America, and they often speak in direct and even violent opposition to emerging generations and cultures.

Over the same period, the more moderate and liberal Protestant mainline has worked to align its social stands with public calls for liberation. I count this as a blessing, since scripture affirms that God is at work wherever people honor one another's human dignity, contribute to common flourishing, and grow in love (1 John 4:7–12). Unfortunately, while members of these churches mastered the language of inclusivity and welcome—Episcopalians are known for our signs announcing "The Episcopal Church Welcomes You"—they were overall more hesitant to engage the public or to venture beyond their founders' Euro-tribal identities, cultural preferences, aesthetics, and worship styles. I don't think these churches always intended to exclude non-dominant groups and cultures. When you love something—especially something bound up with the sacred—it's difficult to imagine why anybody else would not love it, too. In that model, segregation is nearly inevitable.

In the absence of significant efforts on any dominant church's part to meet people where they were *and* to honor God's life in marginalized cultures and spaces, it was only a matter of time until younger and increasingly diverse Americans stopped trying to find a way into these churches' walled-off fortresses. As one millennial shared with my colleague Carrie Boren Headington, an evangelist and racial healing leader in the Diocese of Dallas: "Our workplaces, social hangouts, and even families are much more diverse than the church. Why would we go to church, where we and our friends would not feel comfortable because of its homogeneity? I feel like God is more outside the church than inside."

What does all this mean? If we return to Roxburgh's metaphor of unraveling, we can now see that the tapestry of dominant American Christianity—already full of loose threads—has hopelessly snagged, pulled, and unraveled. Could we simply tuck some threads back in? Roxburgh cautions against easy technical fixes. "Ours is not just any unraveling: it is a great unraveling, for something precious and enormously important to us has come apart and can no longer be woven back together."[12]

Whatever majority American Christianity was it can no longer claim to be. Decline has caused us to spin and unravel. We have entered the wilderness. We've been humbled and unseated. We have cracked open.

Journey to the Cross

All of which brings us to 2020 and the advent of a lethal virus that spreads with particular vigor in crowds, close physical proximity, and wherever people speak, sing, or eat together. In other words: among faith communities.

Early in the spring, congregations began to shut their doors, at first with halting steps, then in great, apocalyptic sweeps. The Lenten readings were in eerie alignment with our lived experience. The third Sunday in Lent, we closed up and followed the Israelites into the wilderness (Exodus 17:1–7). They "quarreled and tested the LORD, saying, 'Is the LORD among us or not?'"—we echoed their plaintive cry. The Israelites complained to Moses and begged for provision; our exhausted leaders and volunteers scrambled to provide worship, pastoral care, and urgent community services without causing more harm than good. The loss of communion was perhaps most keen. Where was our manna? Where was the water of life?

On the fourth Sunday in Lent, March 22, my entire city of New York moved into lockdown. The streets were empty, save the ambulances zooming to overflowing hospitals. The psalm appointed for that day was Psalm 23:

The LORD is my shepherd;
I shall not be in want.
He makes me lie down in green pastures
and leads me beside still waters. . . .
Though I walk through the valley of the shadow of death,
I shall fear no evil;
for you are with me;
your rod and your staff, they comfort me.

It helped, knowing others had trod this path before and found
God to be present and faithful. But it still hurt, not being able to
touch or even breathe together, especially as so many entered the valley of the shadow of death.

On the fifth Sunday of Lent, we watched as Jesus made the sol-
emn journey to visit his dear friend Lazarus, already dead and in the
tomb for four days (John 11). The shortest line in scripture—"Jesus
wept"—was now one of the most meaningful. This Jesus who suffered with his friends, wept with his friends, and loved his friends:
this was the face of God we desperately needed to see.

Holy Week felt more early church than twenty-first century. We
were like those in catacombs, banished from our buildings, gathering and praying in small circles, finding one another online to tell
stories and remember the one we loved. Meals had shades of Jesus's
Last Supper on Maundy Thursday. His loneliness in the garden, just
before the authorities came to take him away, resonated with the iso-
lation of those who would die alone.

Good Friday required no theatrical reenactment. The cross
was everywhere. On the news, in empty sanctuaries, in overflowing
morgues, in households struggling for economic survival, you could
hear the psalmist cry:

My God, my God, why have you forsaken me?
and are so far from my cry
and from the words of my distress? (Psalm 22:1)

And when at last Jesus "bowed his head and gave up his spirit" (John 19:30), we felt the life go out of us. For too many, it would not return.

How we needed Easter in 2020! We needed resurrection, light, and a God who would defeat death once and for all. And while some of us grasped that vibrating strand of hope, I heard friends who have been clergy and church leaders for most of their lives starting to question how they would continue to serve.

Still the pandemic raged. The temporary restrictions became semi-permanent adaptations. Even if we could find a way to sustain financially, could we learn to be church and to be community in such a radically different setting, for an undetermined time? Or was something fundamental about being church and being America falling apart? Was it time to imagine new realities? Jesuit professor Tomás Halík certainly thought so. He wrote in *America* magazine:

> Maybe this time of empty church buildings symbolically exposes the churches' hidden emptiness and their possible future unless they make a serious attempt to show the world a completely different face of Christianity. We have thought too much about converting the world and less about converting ourselves: not simply improvement but a radical change from a static "being Christians" to a dynamic "becoming Christians."[13]

We had invested so much financial, emotional, and spiritual capital in our buildings as the site of the holy (or at least the most intense encounter with the holy) and in the sacraments of Baptism and the Eucharist as the fullest way to receive God's love and spirit. We had communicated—with our actions if not always with our words—that clergy mediation is essential for a sustained connection to God. Could God lead us through a radical re-formation, training us to see and celebrate holiness closer to home, and to trust the laity to develop intimate relationship with God and one another beyond the control of clergy? Now that we could not *go* to church, would we focus on *being* the church?

In a lot of places, the answer has been, "Yes." Churches reported that people who checked out a long time ago had now returned online, because there was less pressure to hold up appearances. Lots of congregations started leaning on younger digital natives who have been waiting for a chance to lead. New networks formed to feed hungry neighbors, and new mission efforts connected with spiritually hungry and lonely people. But the question remained: could we maintain that faithfulness and openness in an extended wilderness sojourn? Or would we minimize the changes and reassemble the cracked pieces in their familiar form as soon as possible?

The Foundations Crumble

The next quake came with the murder of George Floyd on May 25, 2020, and it shook the world, America, and faith communities to the core.

Make no mistake: the anger, agony, and demand for change didn't begin on the streets of Minnesota. State-sponsored and sanctioned violence against Native, Black, Brown, and Asian bodies has been part of the American story longer than there has been an America. At every juncture, we communities of color and our friends have resisted.

Even movement warriors who have been in the trenches since the 1950s and 1960s sensed something different in this crisis. The pain—and the crack in the foundations—ran deeper. If you've seen the video of George Floyd dying, you know why. Death was nothing new. Horrifying as it seems, we had begun to acclimate as a culture to Black death on film. But those numbers: 8 minutes, 46 seconds. His call to his dead mother, "Mama, Mama." His plea, "I can't breathe." It broke through. It broke us.

I wonder if the cracking of the first pandemic broke us open so that we could see and feel afresh the persistent reality of racism and oppression. People heard George Floyd's dying cry in America's cities but also in her small towns and suburbs. They heard him in London, Tokyo, Lusaka, and Bogotá. If you looked at the crowds, you saw people of every race. If you looked a little closer and did the math, at least in the United States, White people often made up the majority.

People of every race gathered brokenhearted to call the names of the dead, and there were so many names to say: Ahmaud Arbery, killed in Georgia by vigilantes who nearly got away without so much as an investigation; Breonna Taylor, an EMT murdered by police who broke into her Louisville home unannounced (Kentucky's attorney general did not press for charges against the officers who killed her); Elijah McClain, a sensitive, violin-playing young Black man murdered by police in Colorado back in 2019 while walking home from the convenience store.

A critical mass of people finally saw the through line between these deaths and mass deportation, anti-Muslim hysteria, mass incarceration, broken treaties, Jim Crow segregation, lynching, anti-Semitism, Japanese internment camps, slavery, Native genocide, Manifest Destiny, and the other evils of racism at the core of American identity and systems. It appeared millions of White people were waking to the ways White supremacy had suffocated and imprisoned their souls, too. Everywhere people recognized the truth others of us have known all along: the "problem" is not people of Black, Indigenous, Latinx, or Asian descent. The "problem" is not division and separation.

The problem is *racism*, "a belief that race is a fundamental determinant of human traits and capacities and that racial differences produce an inherent superiority of a particular race; also the systemic oppression of a racial group to the social, economic, and political advantage of another."[14]

The problem is *White supremacy*. More than hate groups with tiki torches and burning crosses, White supremacy is the ideology, culture, and related systems that together assert the superiority of White ideas, creations, actions, and humanity, thus ensuring the prosperity and domination of White people and White cultures.

The problem is an entire nation founded on the ideology of White supremacy and dedicated to White prosperity and domination—a nation whose existence depends on consuming and discarding the lives and bodies of people of color.

The problem is *Whiteness*. That's not just having White or light-colored skin or even tracing your ancestry to Europe. Whiteness is the umbrella that covers, protects, and elevates light-skinned people (and others it chooses to absorb) while leaving non-White people vulnerable to violence, subjugation, and exploitation. Willie Jennings explains that Whiteness "designates white bodies as the exemplars of beauty, goodness, and truth" and then invites "multiple people(s) to imagine their worlds through white bodies."[15] Note that Whiteness is not the same as racial identity; any person can participate in Whiteness, and any person can resist systems of White racial superiority and domination.

Finally, the problem is churches—particularly those of majority American Christianity—that are declining precisely because they cast their lot with empire, established order, and Whiteness instead of the gospel of Jesus Christ.

This awakening has felt like scales falling, like jars cracking and breaking. It was like Harry Potter and his friends finally saying "Voldemort," the name that shall not be named, but for us the words were "White supremacy," "Whiteness," and "racism." The more we spoke them, the more powerful and free we felt.

But you can't stop with telling the truth and cracking the jar. Between systemic decline, global pandemic, and a historic racial reckoning, the nation and the church were cracked wide open. We could see what rested at the center of the church's life and identity as we never had before. What were we to do with these cracked, broken pieces and the truth they revealed?

The Choice Is Yours

Inertia is the law of physics that says matter will always continue in its current state of rest or motion in a particular direction, unless that state is changed by some outside force. Institutions and cultures are durable partly because they obey the law of inertia. Even if you think you've exerted a strong external push and knocked a moving object or an entire institution off its set course, wait. Just wait. With barely a nudge, the object will drift right back to its original path.

Think of your own experience. When you see a crack, what's your first instinct? Push the pieces back together and patch it over. Eventually a contractor comes with the bad news: there is deep damage here, and if you don't address it, before long the whole structure will be fundamentally compromised. You sigh and negotiate. I don't know about you, but I have a surprising capacity to delude myself about how broken the structure is. With enough duct tape and rope, I will get back to normal.

So it is for a nation and a church. In the midst of displacement, destabilization, and decentering, Americans and church folks have been tempted to replace, restabilize, and recenter. Let's return to the building. Let's encourage the protesters to come off the streets and codify their legislative demands. Let's move past division. Let's reestablish majority American Christianity in its former, privileged cultural post.

Or we could acknowledge the unraveling, breaking, and cracking as a bearer of truth and even a gift. Perhaps, as Roxburgh suggested, the Holy Spirit has been nudging and calling Christians "to embrace a new imagination, but the other one had to unravel for us to see it for what it was. In this sense the malaise of our churches has been the work of God."[16] His words remind me of the text message I shared at this book's outset, the one where I wondered if the church has cracked open and God is behind it all. A church that has been humbled by disruption and decline may be a less arrogant and presumptuous church. It may have fewer illusions about its own power and centrality. It may become curious. It may be less willing to ally with the empires and powers that have long defined it. It may finally admit how much it needs the true power and wisdom of the Holy Spirit. That's a church God can work with.

God did not make our churches shrink, just as God did not willfully spread COVID-19, nor has God compelled the oppression of

Black, Indigenous, Latinx, or Asian peoples, or any other vulnerable groups in this nation. But again and again God turns that which was meant for evil and pain so that it becomes a force capable of saving and healing a multitude (Genesis 50:20).

God took the broken body of God's own son and raised him to new life. God can take these unraveled threads and ragged patches of fabric and knit them into a new tapestry. God can take the cracked pieces of the church, the body of Christ, and fashion a new church with God's purposes at its heart. It will not be the same life or the same body, but a resurrection body that bears the marks of the old and the new.

Disruption and decline are not the end of any story with God. In our case, they may be the doorway into joining God's community of love.

2

New Hope for Beloved Community

*This is the hour of opportunity; this is the hour of the
Church. In the last fifty years she has accomplished a
great preparation, by her rediscovery of the purpose of
Jesus. Few and hesitant, however, have been her attempts
to realize that purpose, to strive boldly, through profound
labors of readjustment and reconstruction, to establish the
Kingdom of God, the kingdom of love, on earth . . .*
—Vida Scudder, The Church and the Hour[1]

People are aching the world over for beloved community. You don't
have to be religious to long for it. There is something elemental
and compelling about communities of people who help one another
to grow into all that they were created to be. Where each person is
as committed to the other's flourishing and to the flourishing of the
whole. Where the members are willing to sacrifice their own comfort
and even lives for the sake of the other and for the dream they share.

You don't have to be religious to seek beloved community. I believe we humans are created with a homing device that begins to hum and light up when we see individuals and communities driven not by ego but by self-giving love.

But if you are religious, and certainly if you are a follower of Jesus Christ, then beloved community should be one of the basic tenets of faith. That's what Jesus told the young seeker who asked him the greatest commandment. Jesus told him, "You shall love the Lord your God with all your heart, and with all your soul, and with all your mind," and "You shall love your neighbor as yourself" (Matthew 22:37–39). Jesus welcomed people into a countercultural, self-giving community of love with God at the center.

True, the ideal gets watered down and starts to resemble a Coca-Cola commercial featuring multi-hued people holding hands and circling the globe. It may also look like "a liberal, multicultural coalition of citizens committed to various strategies of social transformation for the sake of some universal notion of the Good."[2] That's nice, but don't stake your life on it. Instead, hold out for the robust and uncompromising vision of God's kingdom of love. For us, it's a dream. For God, it's reality.

Even if we have failed a thousand times before, don't let this hour pass without calling on Jesus and the prophets one more time. Notice how God's reign is already breaking in and how the Spirit empowers us to join up with that movement. Especially now, even as the powers of empire and established order are busy reassembling the cracked pieces of our national and church life with the same self-centric powers and goals at their core, we should be striving and praying that God will reshape us in the image of God's beloved community. If not now, when?

Pioneers of Beloved Community

Any full reflection on beloved community in this day and age should honor the witness of pioneers like Verna Dozier, Martin Luther King Jr., Dietrich Bonhoeffer, Howard Thurman, Josiah Royce, and Georg

Hegel. Of that group, King is best known for planting beloved community in the modern psyche. As early as 1956, at the end of the Montgomery bus boycott, he pointed protesters to beloved community as their ultimate goal:

> [W]e must remember as we boycott that a boycott is not an end within itself; it is merely a means to awaken a sense of shame within the oppressor and challenge his false sense of superiority. But the end is reconciliation; the end is redemption; the end is the creation of the beloved community. It is this type of spirit and this type of love that can transform opposers into friends. . . . It is this love which will bring about miracles in the hearts of men.[3]

King insisted that the action and reaction on the streets and in the courts should contribute to changed policies, changed hearts, *and* a different way of life for the whole community. Like the prophets before him, he struggled toward a reconciled human family where the miracle of love makes possible what would otherwise be impossible: the end of oppressive systems, the redemption of the oppressor's tainted soul, and true freedom, fellowship, and fullness of life for every child of God. This was the true goal for which they labored and suffered.

In this way, King stood very much in the lineage of leaders like Howard Thurman. A mystic, activist, and scholar, Thurman served as dean of chapel at King's graduate school alma mater, Boston University. In 1936, when King was only a seven-year-old in the pews at Ebenezer Baptist Church in Atlanta, Thurman led a Black delegation to India for an audience with Mahatma Gandhi. They shared about common commitments to nonviolence and civil rights, and that meeting inspired Thurman to craft this generous vision of beloved community:

> There is a spirit abroad in life of which the Judeo-Christian ethic is but one expression. It is a spirit that makes for wholeness and for community . . . it knows no country and its allies are to be

found wherever the heart is kind and the collective will and the private endeavor seek to make justice where injustice abounds, to make peace where chaos is rampant, and to make the voice heard on behalf of the helpless and weak. It is the voice of God and the voice of man; it is the meaning of all the strivings of the whole human race toward a world of friendly men and underneath a friendly sky.[4]

Thurman's picture of "a world of friendly men [and women] and underneath a friendly sky" is way beyond mere tolerance. He aims for a radical reorientation of self to God and to other. Even his use of the word "friendly" indicates a relationship more revolutionary than you might first suspect. Thurman means "friend" the way Jesus meant "friend," as when he said, "No one has greater love than this, to lay down one's life for one's *friends*" (John 15:13, my emphasis). Friends sacrifice and give their lives in order to stop the suffering of those they love. Friends are responsible to the law of heaven (Thurman's "friendly sky") and not the unjust laws of the land. Thurman's world of friendly people underneath a friendly sky is a total reversal of empire, and a fierce embrace of God's beloved community.

King and Thurman both drank deeply from the well of scripture and Black liberation traditions. They also drew on the wisdom of philosophers like Josiah Royce, who is generally credited with first speaking of a "community" of the "beloved."[5] Dig enough, and you will discover Royce relied on the work of Georg Hegel, who spoke in 1831 of the "Kingdom of reconciliation" and "a perfectly lived unity of individual men joined in one divine chorus."[6] Royce took Hegel's thinking a step further when he wrote: "In the Kingdom you, and your enemy, and yonder stranger, are one. For the Kingdom is the community of God's beloved."[7]

Royce envisioned a nonexclusive community saturated in practical, devoted love. He understood this love as "loyalty,"[8] and he insisted it could be extended to another person or small group, to a community, or to a shared cause. Eventually, it might become so "maximally inclusive" that it would embrace and honor even people not in its circle.[9] For him, that was the realization of beloved community.

Not that Royce actually expected people to create such communities on their own. We're human. We hurt each other, often without even trying. After the community has sustained some wound or injustice, a rift opens. The only way to make it right, and to knit the community back together, is through atonement. What is that? *Atonement is an act of spiritual sacrifice or reparation undertaken by an individual or group, almost as a gift to the community as a whole.*[10] This self-giving act shocks the conscience of the opponent so much it cracks them open and makes way for God's spirit to intercede. Atonement effects the spiritual alchemy that turns their hearts of stone to flesh.

If this sounds confusing or otherworldly, just picture the witness of nonviolent resistance. Recall Jesus turning the other cheek, Gandhi going on hunger strike, or Fannie Lou Hamer sitting in a Mississippi jail cell. These practitioners of confrontational nonviolence chose to make extraordinary spiritual and physical sacrifices. Why? Because they trusted that if they resisted violence and looked at their opponents with God's peace and soul-power, the victimizer would be so ashamed, so shocked with conscience, he would cease the harmful behavior. More than that, he might reevaluate his own identity and reality, and question why he ever thought himself superior or separate from the oppressed one before him. He might eventually pledge his own life to the nonviolent way of love and join in beloved community.

Neither Royce, Thurman, nor King expected any group to achieve this ideal, reconciled state, but they all trusted the striving would make life worth living. Giving up hope was simply not an option.

I am reminded here of Verna Dozier, a Black Episcopal laywoman and theologian who also stood firmly at the intersection of harsh reality and divine hope. She was the first to admit, "The world is not as God would have it." But she went on: "The kingdoms of this world are not yet the kingdom of God, but they can become it. They are not yet the realm where God's sovereignty is acknowledged and lived out, but they can become it."[11]

That mix of longing and pragmatism informs my own church's teaching on beloved community today. When the Episcopal Church made a public, long-term commitment to racial healing, reconciliation, and justice in 2017, we titled it "Becoming Beloved Community." Not "Being" but "Becoming." We understood that beloved community is the enactment of the reign of God, which means it is at once a compelling reality and a distant hope. It beckons as God's preferred future, the bright beacon we see through fog and rain, inspiring and guiding our next, best steps toward home. We may not get there, but we know God has already prepared it.

God's Love in the Flesh

Beloved community is God's vision for creation. So if you want to see this concept enfleshed, look to the community God created when he walked among us. Look to Jesus of Nazareth.

Jesus never used the phrase "beloved community"; he just built one. That mythic group of disciples, a cadre of misfits who grew to love God, each other, and the world as much as they loved their own individual lives, has inspired film, literature, social movements, and human life for two millennia and counting. Give me the Avengers, the Justice League, or the Bad News Bears, and I'll show you how they resemble Jesus's beloved community.

Jesus purposefully gathered insiders and outsiders, scandalous women and illiterate men, hungry children and wealthy benefactors, all of whom had only begun to understand their own brokenness and need. He told them they were grafted onto one vine. When they tried to make it all about him, he turned their attention to God and to one another. When they obsessed over which of them was the greatest, he knelt and washed their feet.

We tend to make beloved community complicated, probably so we can create loopholes to slip away from the sacrifice and challenge such a life entails. Jesus consistently untangled the complications and offered simple, earth-shattering messages like: "This is my commandment, that you love one another as I have loved you" (John 15:12). He followed up those words by dying between two criminals, his arms stretched on the hard wood of the cross, the very picture of love, pain, forgiveness, and solidarity.

The apostle Paul had more than his share of hang-ups, including his desire to make following Jesus palatable to his own insider, Greek-speaking, Jewish culture. But even Paul was converted toward Jesus's call to become a beloved community, where the first are last and the last are first, and where our differences are still present but no longer indicate hierarchy. How? "[I]n the one Spirit we were all baptized into one body—Jews or Greeks, slaves or free—and we were all made to drink of one Spirit" (1 Corinthians 12:13). Once they were baptized and clothed with Christ, the game had changed. There was no longer slave or free (or more pointedly, slave *against* free, or slave *below* free). In Christ, those who were once far and those who were once near now stand on equal footing.

You can imagine the privileged community members pulled Paul aside, reminded him of their status, and insisted they would be better off in a special, separate section for people like them. Paul quickly closed that door. "[T]he body does not consist of one member but of many," he told the Corinthians. "If the foot would say, 'Because I am not a hand, I do not belong to the body,' that would not make it any less a part of the body (1 Corinthians 12:14–15). Self-sufficiency is actually a deficiency in the context of beloved community. If you think you could get by on your own, it means you still don't understand what God is creating. If you think every other member of the body should be like you, a basic assumption in an empire, then you've missed the glorious diversity, complexity, and interdependence God built into creation.

In beloved community, nobody is inferior or superior, of greater or lesser value. "The eye cannot say to the hand, 'I have no need of you,' nor again the head to the feet, 'I have no need of you.' On the contrary, the members of the body that seem to be weaker are indispensable" (vv. 21–22). Not only do the powerful not get to lord it over others, but in God's community of love the ones on the bottom matter even more. Think of it as divine affirmative action. Because the world has cast certain groups down, God provides the extra honor necessary to balance those wrongs and achieve equity. Their experiences become gifts to the whole. Their suffering and persecution yield a precious store of wisdom, vulnerability, and compassion. To God and to a God-centered community, the world's oppressed and humiliated peoples are truly essential.

Embracing the Cracks

The powerful and privileged will find this a tough lesson to learn and an even more difficult one to live by. Maybe that's why it is so hard for a rich man to enter the kingdom of heaven—harder than it is for a camel to squeeze through the eye of a needle (Matthew 19:24). It's probably why the rich young man turned away when Jesus invited him to give up everything for the sake of the poor and follow Jesus (Matthew 19:16–22). He did not know how to survive without his possessions and position, not just because of greed, but because they defined him. Jesus offered to train him out of self-centric and self-seeking behaviors, toward self-giving and self-emptying. The young man did not want that freedom or ultimately that joy. Most human beings don't.

The word for this counterintuitive, descending movement is *kenosis*, and it has everything to do with beloved community. It comes from the Greek *kenos*, which means "empty," so kenosis is basically the act of emptying oneself. In theological terms, it refers to Jesus's willing renunciation (or emptying himself) of pure divinity in order to also become incarnate as a human being, to live and love as one of us, and ultimately to suffer the death of one who is despised. I could say more here about kenosis, but it is so central to being cracked open to becoming beloved community that we will spend chapter 6 on it.

When I envision kenosis in service of beloved community, I picture the Acts community: people from every walk of life and culture sharing their gifts so that no one had less or more than they needed.

If you had more faith, you shared with those who had less. If you had more money, it went into the common pot so everyone had enough. If you had great knowledge, you should be teaching others. And you used your power to protect the most vulnerable. That unlikely body of Jesus's followers prayed, ate, and sang together at home and in the temple courts, filling the air with praise for God, sharing good news and love with their neighbors in a way that was so contagious and life-giving, others couldn't wait to take up this countercultural, self-giving way for themselves (Acts 2:42–47). That beloved community was so compelling and contagious, people around them exclaimed, "Who are these people who are so full of love?"

Postcolonial theologian Christopher Duraisingh says this is the true arc of the gospel. God hasn't called us to build a new Tower of Babel, where all people gather in one place, speaking one language. Neither does God call us to be "self-sufficient, discrete and bounded selves" standing apart, like segregated figures who cannot interact, touch, or change.[12] Instead, Duraisingh says, God's movement looks like Pentecost, where communities and individuals discover the blessing of being "permeable, open to the other, mutual and multivoiced." As we bring many voices, languages, and gifts into mutually transforming community, everybody is changed and enriched.[13]

I want that life for myself, for the church, and for the world. And I know the only way we step from our small circles of safety and homogeneity, and into a new circle filled with deep discomfort, challenge, and holiness, is through love.

Love Is the Way

The word "love" gets used so often by such disparate voices that it risks meaning nothing at all. Still, love is the only way to define the force that awakens and animates beloved community. I would rather we reclaim it than bury it.

One reason to hold onto love is because love rests at the heart of God. It *is the heart of God*, beating and aching and drawing near to us in Jesus. John 3:16 affirms this truth: "For God so loved the world that he gave his only Son, so that everyone who believes in him may not perish but may have eternal life." Pause and linger with the first part: "God so loved the world he gave his only son." Those words—*loved* and *gave*—they speak to something essential about God. What does love do? Love gives its own life for the sake of the beloved. How do we know God is love? Because, in Jesus, God gives God's own self away.

So yes, Paul was right in 1 Corinthians 13. Love *is* patient and kind. It does not boast, insist on getting its own way, or set its needs ahead of the needs of others. It bears and forgives all things, and it can endure all things. Love seeks and invests in the flourishing of the other. Loves gives its own life away. We know because God first loved us.

Now imagine that love stretched out, from you to me, from us to others. Watch as it enfolds not just a few people, not just a family, not just a racial group, not just a nation. Imagine it encompassing enemies, the whole human family, and the whole of God's good creation.

While only God expresses this love perfectly, we've been invited to join and share in it. By the power of the Spirit, we stretch and discover the blessing of giving and loving. Of course, we then get anxious and grabby and fall down. Full of grace and forgiveness, God scrapes us off the floor, reminds us of the power of love, and welcomes us to open to the breadth and power of God's love yet again.

Beloved community is the community animated by this nonclinging, self-emptying, persistent love. It seeks wholeness and kindness, as the individual and the collective strive and sacrifice for the sake of the flourishing of the greater whole and for the end of all forms of domination and oppression that diminish the children of God. If I am constantly bowing to you and you are bowing to me—if I am truly your friend and you are mine—then we will both flourish. If we join God in nourishing and fostering that mutual regard everywhere, God's creation could become a community of love.

3

The Origins of the Nightmare

*[B]efore the doctor will even see you, he wants to know
your history. He doesn't want to know just your history,
he wants to know your mother's history. He wants to
know your father's history. They may go back to your
grandmother and your grandfather on both sides. . . . You
cannot diagnose a problem until you know the history of
the problem that you're trying to resolve. I think that it's
not as hard as . . . you might fear it will be, that actually
you can find it, not just enlightening, but healing.*

—Isabel Wilkerson[1]

H istory matters. Your history, my history, our history: these stories make us what we are. To hold out a realistic and renewed
hope for beloved community, to see the actual distance between
that ideal and the current state of dis-ease in the United States

35

and in dominant American Christian communities, we have to tell America's truth.

As readers, you will come to this moment of disruption, decline, and reckoning from different starting places. Some people are in a state of discovery, and the contours of America's long identification with empire and domination—and the deep complicity of faith communities—will come as a painful revelation. Phrases like "White supremacy" may seem out of place, even when we deemphasize the swastikas and define it as an ideology, culture, and accompanying structures that privilege White identity, assume White superiority in virtually all facets of society, and subjugate non-White peoples and cultures. If you need to pause, wrestle, or rest with your own responses, I hope you'll take that time. *The Church Cracked Open* Reflection & Action Guide should prove helpful, especially if you'd like even more backstory and reflection prompts.

Others have been in the trenches and will find the accounts that follow woefully familiar. I hope there's some gift for you, too, especially as you think about how you can help others learn and reckon with these stories.

Wherever you start, I pray we all eventually arrive at a place of shared urgency and conviction. This is no time to tinker at the church's edges or to put the cracked pieces back together as they were. Something essential needs to be recognized and emptied from this nation and its majority-identified churches in order for God's life to become our life. To do that soul-level work, we have to go back to the histories and stories of our parents and grandparents and further still. How did a nation founded to be a holy city on a hill fall so very far into the valley? Let's engage that question now, trusting Jesus who said, "you shall know the truth and the truth shall set you free" (John 8:32).

Self-Centrism: The Root of Original Sin

Jewish and Hindu teachers alike relate a fable about two dinner parties. One party is in hell, the other in heaven. At both parties, the tables are laden with yummy food. Both tables have the same long spoons for eating. In hell, the diners are starving, while in heaven, they're feasting.

What's the difference? In hell, diners try to serve themselves, but it's impossible to position their own hands to guide the food to their own mouths. In heaven, they feed each other. Your long spoon reaches perfectly to feed someone across the table. Another person's long spoon lifts food to your mouth. All are fed.

Beloved community looks and acts like that heavenly banquet. The United States in particular—despite its extraordinary gifts and stated values—looks very little like that beloved community. Shaken by a historic pandemic, unmasked White supremacy, and the seeming triumph of cultures of consumerism, materialism, and individualism, the case could be made that we resemble something closer to a nightmare.

How did we get here? You have to begin at the beginning. According to Genesis 1 and 2, each and every one of us was created in God's image. We were made by God out of love to be in relationship with God and each other. In other words, we were made by love for love. That's in our DNA.

At the heart of love is the ability to choose. If the love was forced or mandated, then it wouldn't be love. Given the choice, human beings tend to turn from God's way of self-giving love, and instead choose to construct worlds that revolve around self: our needs, our identities, our desires. This turning from God is sin. More specifically, the term I will use throughout this book is self-centrism. That's different from self-centeredness, which means I am centered on myself. Self-centrism is an orientation in relation to the world that assumes I am at the center and the world rotates around me (or my group, my nation, my race, my kind), so that everything and everyone else has meaning or value only insofar as it serves the self at the center.

We humans seem to be wired for self-centrism as individuals, as family groups, as communities, and indeed as races and nations. I would not say we emerge from the womb wishing others ill or thinking we're the only ones who matter. Rather, it seems we harbor an original terror that we are not wanted or welcome on this earth, and that if we do not value and protect ourselves or our group, no one else will . . . not even God.

Priest and prophet Henri Nouwen brings insight and compassion to this soft spot at the heart of human existence. I keep a set of his daily meditations by my bed. In one, he writes:

> Not being welcome is your greatest fear. It connects with your birth fear, your fear of not being welcome in this life, and your death fear, your fear of not being welcome in the life after this. It is the deep-seated fear that it would have been better if you had not lived. . . . You have to choose life. At every moment you have to decide to trust the voice that says, "I love you. I knit you together in your mother's womb."[2]

This is one of the most common threads in scripture: we don't trust we are beloved, even as God reassures us that we can choose life and trust the God who made us in love and for love. We still don't believe there's enough love to go around, so God tries to free us from this deep-seated fear so we can participate in extending love with one another. God's love simply will not run out; if anything, the supply grows as we share it.

In Deuteronomy 10:17–19, God patiently reminds the Israelites of all the ways God protected and provided for them when they were strangers making a treacherous wilderness sojourn out of slavery: "You shall also love the stranger, for you were strangers in the land of Egypt." Trust me, God seems to beg them. Out of my own generosity and love, I have given you life. Now I need you to guard, provide for, and honor the strangers, aliens, and other vulnerable people in your midst. I need you to give your life away.

In Jesus, God renounces the privilege of divinity and distance in order to dwell, identify, and suffer with us, particularly those of us on the underside. As God among us, he issues the direct invitation to place God at the center of our lives, to see God in ourselves and others, and to celebrate and safeguard their belovedness, too (Matthew 22:36–40). Preaching this message landed Jesus in heaps of trouble. At the very start of his ministry, Jesus walked into the temple and announced God had sent him to bring good news to the poor and set the captives free (Luke 4:16–20). The crowds cheered . . . until Jesus explained that included non-Jews. Then the same crowd tried to throw him off a cliff (Luke 4:25–29).

Jesus kept preaching that truth because he knew our self-centric instincts—left unchecked—would prevent us ever having right relationship with God and one another and would likely place the world in peril.

Us against You

And so it is today. When you see cultures based on White supremacy, misogyny, environmental exploitation, consumerism, oppression, and domination, you are actually seeing the fallout from self-centrism. Entire systems, institutions, and societies are fully capable of this sin, as when a group places itself at the center and expects the rest of humanity and creation to support its singular prosperity.

There is no possibility for right relationship if one powerful group protects and sustains itself over *and against* all others. From there, it's just too easy to construct binaries and hierarchies of human existence. Our group is good; all of you are bad. Our group belongs on top; we have to keep you low. Our group owns these resources and knows the best way to use them; you will only receive what we give you. Other members of the human family become objects and tools to be acquired, controlled, used, and discarded.

I once asked a straight, White, middle-class, male friend to just talk to me about how he understands these hierarchies and the emotional and personal motivations behind them. "When you've been told something is yours," he shared, "part of you believes it, whether it's possessions, position, or an identity. There's something in you that needs to have it and keep it. If it's threatened or limited in any way, you fear your own existence is at risk. You'll do what you have to do to protect and keep it for yourself and for each other. It's what every human group would instinctively do, if they were the ones on top. Right?"

That may be true about humanity (for the record, I am not convinced it is). If so, it explains why many of us need Jesus and the Spirit-powered movement he founded to snap us out of our self-seeking spiral. It may also be that "every human group" would do the same, but for at least five hundred years a particular race, gender, and economic class have consistently followed the call of self-centrism, with deadly consequences for those not in their circles.

Self-centrism is the force that powers empire and colonialism. As we saw in chapter 1, *empire* is one country exercising power over another country, through colonial settlement but also through military domination, political sovereignty, or indirect means of control; while *colonialism* is one country taking control of another by occupying it with settlers and exploiting it economically.

How are these related to what I call self-centrism? Postcolonial theologian Christopher Duraisingh uses a metaphor from physics to make the point. "The colonial power has been primarily centripetal, in drawing all that is at its periphery to the center for the sole benefit of the center," he explains. "It has bifurcated the world into the West and the rest."[3]

You can actually picture what Duraisingh describes here. In calling the colonial power *centripetal*, he means it is self-centric: it rotates and generates a force that draws all the resources and power inward toward the center. It's the opposite of a *centrifugal* force, which is created when an object spins and everything around it flushes to the edges. Still with me? Close your eyes and imagine the relationship of planets and other celestial bodies to the sun. Centripetal force keeps them from flying off in a billion directions, and instead orients them so they orbit around the sun.

Self-centrism places me and my needs at the center and sets the world in motion around me. Colonialism and White supremacy have centered one group of people—the conqueror, White people, light-skinned people whose bloodlines trace primarily to northern Europe—and then organized the other peoples and resources of the world in inferior, dependent relation to that center. In this way, "the rest" of the earth's lands and bodies have been pressed into submission and service to "the West."

The Age of Conquest

As I've noted, you would be hard-pressed to find a race, culture, generation, or gender that doesn't struggle with the temptation toward self-centrism. At the same time, there is no denying that European nations and their descendants, especially the United States, are unique in the breadth and totality of their self-centric, narcissistic domination of the rest of the globe. The cracking open we have experienced over the last few years, and more intensely starting in 2020, is in part because more people are naming these truths.

We can thank scholars like Roxanne Dunbar-Ortiz for shining the light and fueling that reckoning. She won the American Book Award in 2015 for *An Indigenous People's History of the United States.* In this tour-de-force, she flings aside the veil and retells American history from the perspective of the Native peoples who were originally present and thriving across the continent, only to be displaced and slaughtered by European conquest.

Dunbar-Ortiz claims the machine that ravaged Africa and the Americas was actually set in motion in the eleventh through the thirteenth centuries.[4] During that time, European crusaders set out to conquer North Africa and the Middle East. Toward the end of the thirteenth century, fueled by a desire for even more riches, the popes directed crusaders to also crush their enemies closer to home: pagans, heretics, and any commoners who resisted their rule in places like Scotland, Wales, Ireland, and the Basque Country.

The process was simple and devastating: conquerors would sweep through and brutalize their opponents (the English paid tribute for severed heads in their campaigns against the Irish and then displayed them on pikes[5]). They forced conquered peoples off their land, compelled them to work to produce wealth for the conquering nation and its nobility, erased their culture and Indigenous sources of identity and power, and trapped them in dependent relationship to the colonial ruler.

In time, the popes and monarchs joined forces to colonize new lands. Pope Nicholas V issued the papal bull *Dum Diversas* in 1452 to provide the king of Portugal with an explicit charge to convert, subdue, enslave, and if necessary slaughter Muslims, pagans, and any other non-Christians in West Africa.[6] In 1455, with the bull *Romanus Pontifex*, the same pope authorized the Catholic nations of Europe to extend their dominion as far as the winds would carry them. These papal bulls and related statements are collectively known as the <u>Doctrine of Discovery</u>, and they functioned as the firing gun that launched the colonization of most of the non-European world between the mid-fifteenth and mid-twentieth centuries.[7]

Reading the papal bulls and the writings that accompanied them, it is impossible to ignore the self-centric, imperial drive to harness power and wealth around the globe and route it back to Europe. Cloaked with the language of faith, the decrees bless the powerful to dominate all that they survey and destroy the rest. Pope Nicholas V expressed his personal desire to "bring the sheep entrusted to him by God into the single divine fold." Nearly every depraved act that followed could be justified under this holy banner:

> [W]e bestow suitable favors and special graces on those Catholic kings and princes, who, like athletes and intrepid champions of the Christian faith . . . not only restrain the savage excesses of the Saracens and of other infidels, enemies of the Christian name, but also . . . vanquish them and their kingdoms and habitations, though situated in the remotest parts unknown to us, and subject them to their own temporal dominion.[8]

The English watched as Spain and Portugal grew rich through conquest. In 1496, England's King Henry VII accorded similar permission to legendary explorer John Cabot to stake a claim for the English. As an agent of the crown, Cabot could take any lands he found, as long as the Spanish or Portuguese hadn't claimed them first. In exchange, Cabot promised to give the king one-fifth of the value of whatever he brought back to England.[9]

The peoples in these "discovered" lands had no understanding of the machinations swirling in Europe, nor did they have much hope of resisting the onslaught of European guns, germs, and steel.[10] Perhaps to soothe the European conscience, colonizers sometimes read statements to the Indigenous peoples explaining the settlers' purpose. One example is the *Requerimiento* ("Requirement"). In this extraordinary letter, read on behalf of the Spanish monarch, the conquerors declared (1) the Lord their God created all people in the whole world; (2) the same God appointed Saint Peter "to be superior to all the other people of the world . . . the head of the entire human race, wherever men might exist"; (3) St. Peter's power and dominion passed through the line of the popes; and (4) the current pope granted the monarch and his successors control over the lands and seas the Indigenous peoples currently occupied.[11]

The *Requerimiento* did not aim for conversion; its goal was submission. If the Indigenous peoples refused to recognize the monarch's authority, or even if they delayed, the consequences were dire:

> [W]ith the aid of God, we will enter your land against you with force and will make war in every place and by every means we can and are able, and we will then subject you to the yoke and authority of the Church and Their Highnesses. We will take you and your wives and children and make them slaves, and as such we will sell them, and will dispose of you and them as Their Highnesses order. And we will take your property and will do to you all the harm and evil we can. . . . We avow that the deaths and harm which you will receive thereby will be your own blame.

The *Requerimiento* reads like a blueprint for European conquest and destruction. True to their word, the Spanish, Portuguese, French,

Dutch, and English traveled the globe; claimed land, resources, and human lives on behalf of God and the crown; and did "all the harm and evil" they could with few consequences and little moral compunction.

In the case of British conquest, the settlers sent to establish a foothold and war against the Indigenous peoples were the very displaced peoples of Scotland, Ireland, and other European nations who had been abused and defeated centuries earlier. Dunbar-Ortiz notes the irony for us. "The traumatized souls thrown off the land, as well as their descendants, became the land-hungry settlers enticed to cross a vast ocean with the promise of land and attaining the status of gentry."[12] They had learned the logic of conquest the hard way and were determined this time to come out on top. The Scots-Irish who had been victimized by the English became settler-colonizers and scalp collectors in the Americas. If it took the extermination of Indigenous peoples and the enslavement of generations of Africans, that was the ticket guaranteeing their own success and security.

One (White) Nation under God

If there were such a thing as a "ticket" into American prosperity and insider-status, it would be stamped "White." The Irish and other light-skinned European groups didn't necessarily start out with that ticket, but if they proved they were willing to serve the White Anglo-Saxon center, and if they helped to enforce systems that excluded and subjugated Indigenous, Black, and other non-European peoples, then they could gain admittance into *Whiteness*, the identity that White supremacy culture created to house everyone who is to be protected and privileged on the basis of light skin color. (To explore this topic more, see the Reflection & Action Guide.) They didn't instantly get all the benefits—those privileges were still reserved for people of a certain class and pedigree—but at least they were inside. Once inside, they could be trusted to protect the self-centric, racial hierarchies at America's core.

Where did this notion of one racial group at the center or the top of humanity even come from? Able scholars have traced the development of racial categorization in human society; I am particularly indebted to the work of Kelly Brown Douglas, who writes extensively on the topic in *Stand Your Ground: Black Bodies and the Justice of God.* I've gathered some key insights, and those of others, in the accompanying Reflection & Action Guide. But it is still worth spending time now exploring how racial categories have been used to sort humanity into hierarchies of being and, in particular, to place Whiteness at the top of the heap.

Most narratives about White superiority and Whiteness start with Tacitus, a Roman politician and historian who was beloved among the men who shaped early American thought and life, including Ben Franklin, Thomas Jefferson, and John Adams. Tacitus, who died in AD 120, had written about the Germanic tribes (not to be confused with modern Germans) who faced off against the Roman empire in the first century. With almost fawning admiration, he says they were "a distinct unmixed race, like none but themselves."[13] Untainted by intermarriage, their Anglo-Saxon blood was as pure as their principles, and they were uniquely dedicated to individual rights and liberty.

The English claimed they were descended from these high-minded, ancient Anglo-Saxon Germanic tribes.[14] Colonial leaders in America, hardly known for their purity of blood, went on to make the shocking claim that they were the true descendants of the fierce, intelligent, virtuous, industrious, liberty-loving Anglo-Saxons.

The settlers and leaders in America pursued their noble cause: to establish a holy, free, and prosperous city on a hill, one marked by Anglo-Saxon identity and ideals. The idea that Black and Indigenous people should enjoy the same rights and dignity as Whites in this exceptional city would have been inconceivable. These darker peoples had been provided by God as the tools to build the city, not as its citizens. Nothing else made sense to Ben Franklin, who wrote in 1751:

[T]he Number of purely white People in the World is proportion-
ably very small. All *Africa* is black or tawny; *Asia* chiefly tawny;
America (exclusive of the new Comers) wholly so. And in *Europe*,
the *Spaniards, Italians, French, Russians,* and *Swedes,* are generally of what we call a swarthy Complexion; as are the *Germans*
also, the *Saxons* only excepted, who, with the *English*, make the
principal Body of White People on the Face of the Earth. I could
wish their Numbers were increased. And while we are, as I may
call it, *Scouring* our Planet, by *clearing America* of Woods, and
so making this Side of our Globe reflect a brighter Light to the
Eyes of Inhabitants in *Mars* or *Venus*, why should we, in the
Sight of Superior Beings, darken its People? Why increase the
Sons of *Africa*, by planting them in *America*, where we have so
fair an Opportunity, by excluding all Blacks and Tawneys, of
increasing the lovely White and Red*? But perhaps I am partial
to the Complexion of my Country, for such Kind of Partiality is
natural to Mankind. . . . The people who inhabit the nation are
the measure of its purity.[15]

Franklin's words about "purity" and "the lovely White" sound as
if they were pulled straight from a White nationalist manual and not
written by one of the signers of the Declaration of Independence.
It bears repeating that America *was* founded to be a White nation.
If it included non-White people, especially the "Sons of Africa,"
they were present only for what they contributed to the birth of this
exceptional White land. At the time Franklin wrote these words *and
for most of American history*, the assumption of White supremacy

---

*The "red" people Franklin refers to were not Indigenous peoples, who
would have been classified as "tawny." The red race might have included
Russians, Central Asians, and others related to the Caucasus region. For
more, see Georges-Louis Leclerc Buffon (1707–88), father of the modern
concept of race and author of *Natural History of the Globe, and of Man,
Beasts, Birds, Fishes, Reptiles, and Insects.*

and superiority and the related inferiority and disposability of other groups in the human family would have been accepted fact for people of European descent.

Nearly a hundred years later, in the spirit of Franklin, Senator Thomas Hart Benton of Missouri offered a compelling and comprehensive case for the superiority and centrality of the White race around the globe and particularly in America. Addressing the Senate in 1846, he stated matter-of-factly:

> It would seem that the White race alone received the divine command, to subdue and replenish the earth! For it is the only race that has obeyed it, the only one that hunts out new and distant lands, and even a New World, to subdue and replenish. Starting from western Asia, taking Europe for their field, and the Sun for their guide, and leaving Mongolians behind, they arrived, after many ages, on the shores of the Atlantic, which they lit up with the lights of science and religion, and adorned with the useful and elegant arts. Three and half centuries ago, this race, in obedience to the great command, arrived in the New World, and found new lands to subdue and replenish. . . . Civilisation, or extinction, has been the fate of all people who have found themselves in the track of the advancing Whites, and civilisation, always the preference of the Whites, has been pressed as an object, while extinction has followed as a consequence of its resistance. The black and the Red race have often felt their ameliorating [improving] influence.[16]

Benton presented the sweeping evidence of White conquest as proof of White superiority. It was clear to Benton that God had selected and blessed White people, placed them at the center, and given them the power to subdue the other peoples and lands of the globe for their own benefit. If other races possessed the scientific, religious, artistic, and overall intellectual prowess of Whites, they could have done the same. That they did not or could not only proved White people's election by God.

Once he made that case, Benton assumed non-White people have one of two choices: civilization (that is, assimilation or compelled participation in European and Euro-American–dominated systems) or extinction. True to the logic of the White colonial project, all things on earth would be drawn into the White orbit, to be used or discarded as White people see fit.

Connect the Dots

How did we come to 2020 in America? Why, in a nation so rich, are the life chances of Indigenous, Black, Latinx, and Asian people so diminished? Why have a disproportionate number of people of color died in the coronavirus pandemic? Why are we still being lynched in broad daylight? Why is Sunday morning still so segregated, even as our schools and neighborhoods re-segregate? The sad truth is that America is doing exactly what America was designed to do. This nation was not originally designed to be a place where non-White people, as a whole, would thrive, live fully free, or be recognized as fully human. That reality has been challenged and has at times gone underground, but it has never, ever disappeared.

Yes, the Declaration of Independence famously asserts that "all men are created equal" and that "they are endowed by their Creator with certain unalienable rights." For a long time, that canopy did not cover non-White people, women, or men without property. Internal contradictions like this are a hallmark of the American story. We received the world's struggling peoples and gave them a shot at life, but we also exploited and oppressed immigrants. Likewise, Christians brought fervent prayer, strong conviction, and self-giving love to the center of the abolitionist movement; church leaders also wrote some of the most compelling justifications for slavery and the apartheid regime known as Jim Crow. Our history is far from one-sided or simple, and I am grateful for the strands of light and silk woven among the thorns. They tell me redemption is possible, even if it is not a foregone conclusion.

The truth is, Franklin's and Benton's perspectives resemble the bulk of American law and history, stretched over the centuries. They explain Manifest Destiny, the American myth that European-descended settler-colonizers were destined by God to expand and rule across North America. They also illustrate how White supremacy, individualism, colonialism, and domination have colored every element of the great American experiment, including its churches.

It would take another book—volumes of them—to unspool the full story of empire and White domination and how it has formed America into the antithesis of God's beloved community. The Reflection & Action Guide includes a fuller timeline and additional resources for those who wish to do a deeper dive. In the limited space in this chapter, I will point to a few significant markers, so we can better connect the dots and recognize the depth of America's commitment to the nightmare.

- 1490s: The land later known as the United States is home to at least ten million as many as fifty million people in various Indigenous nations. By 1890, it is home to only 249,000.[17]
- 1787: The U.S. Constitutional Convention arrives at the Three-fifths Compromise. Leaders were torn over how to count slaves when deciding each state's legislative representation and tax burden. They finally reach a compromise: count three out of every five slaves (or each slave is 3/5 of a human being).
- 1830: President Andrew Jackson signs the Indian Removal Act, giving the government power to negotiate the exchange of Indigenous land east of the Mississippi (valuable cotton-producing territory) for an "Indian colonization zone" in what is now Oklahoma. Jackson and his successor Martin Van Buren later defy the law and forcibly remove tribes. The 1,200-mile trek west—often called the Trail of Tears—killed up to one-quarter of the tens of thousands of Indigenous peoples expelled from their own lands.[18]

- 1857: The U.S. Supreme Court denies Dred Scott's plea for freedom after his master (now deceased) brought him into free territories. Chief Justice Roger Taney asserts in the majority opinion that Black people could make no claim on liberty because they have "for more than a century before been regarded as beings of an inferior order, and altogether unfit to associate with the white race, either in social or political relations; and so far inferior, that they had no rights which the white man was bound to respect."[19]

- 1859: New York Harbor outfits 85 slave ships responsible for transporting 30,000–60,000 slaves annually, generating enormous profits for New York's merchants and labor for New York's households and businesses.[20]

- 1865: The Thirteenth Amendment abolishes slavery, except in the case of prisoners. The period known as Reconstruction begins, and Black people can at last own land, vote, marry, and breathe freely.

- 1866: White supremacy reasserts itself in the form of Jim Crow laws, such as the one in the state of Mississippi declaring "[A]ll freedmen, free Negroes, and mulattoes in this state over the age of eighteen years, found . . . with no lawful employment or business, or found unlawfully assembling themselves together, either in the day or night time . . . shall be deemed vagrants."[21]

- 1875–1943: Congress consistently blocks the doors to Asian immigration[22] by passing laws that excluded or abridged Asian immigration and citizenship, starting in 1875 with the Page Act, which prohibited "undesirable" immigrants (especially "Coolie" Chinese labor on the West Coast) and peaking in 1924 with the Johnson-Reed Act, which prevented immigration from Asia; reduced immigration from eastern, central, and southern Europe by 80 percent; set immigration quotas based on the census; and established the U.S. Border Patrol.

- 1906: President Theodore Roosevelt shares his fear that Whites are committing "race suicide" by ignoring the disparities between the birthrates of "old stock" immigrants (from America's original source nations like England and Scotland, and even Ireland and Germany) and "new stock" immigrants (Eastern Europeans and a smattering of Asians).[23]

- 1930s: President Franklin Delano Roosevelt engineers the largest mass deportation of immigrants in U.S. history by expelling hundreds of thousands (possibly up to two million) people of Mexican descent. Many of the deportees are American citizens.[24]

- 1910s–1970: States institute literacy tests and other strategies to prevent Black people exercising their right to vote. The Voting Rights Act in 1965 ends the practice in targeted states. Literacy tests do not end nationwide until 1970.[25]

- Today: At the United States southern border, refugees from Latin America are detained, separated child from parent, and held in subhuman conditions for months on end. Unaccompanied minors must defend themselves in courts of law, with the unsurprising result that 71 percent of cases result in deportation.[26]

- Today: Native lands are taken, sacred burial sites are destroyed, environmental concerns and treaties are ignored by U.S. representatives, and children are removed from their parents' homes and placed with White families across America. Oglala County, South Dakota, home of the Pine Ridge Reservation, is the poorest county in the U.S. and has a male life expectancy of forty-seven, thirty years less than the national average.[27] In 2020, Native people have the highest rate of COVID-19 death[28] and the greatest chance of being killed by the police.[29]

- Today: Former and current police officers kill unarmed Black people like Ahmaud Arbery, Breonna Taylor, and George Floyd (and others whose deaths will be logged after I write these words), while White militias roam the streets with military-grade firearms under the approving eye of the authorities.

- Today: The United States has no anti-lynching law on the books. Although the House passed new legislation in 2018, the Senate has not adopted it.

Awake and Aware

We should hold onto God's promise of beloved community. We should give thanks whenever that reality breaks in with beauty and power, as it has at different points in history (some of which we'll see in chapter 5). We should pray to God for wholeness and mutual flourishing, and labor for it alongside other committed souls. We should draw on the strength and witness of ancestors who clung to hope in their day and could not have imagined the freedoms many of us experience in ours.

We should also operate with a keen awareness of the historic, systemic forces and structures built to prevent the plan of God and the dream of the ancestors from becoming real. We have to steel ourselves to peer into the heart of empire and into the ancient, White supremacist myths that formed and still shape America. We have to call sin by its name if we long to be free and if we hope to remake a church, nation, and world that are not rooted in domination systems.

Sin is placing yourself or your group at the center where God belongs and advancing yourself or your group at the expense of others. White supremacy, colonialism, economic exploitation, consumerism, and individualism participate in sin because together they assert that creation should serve not God's purposes but the purpose of the self and the powerful. These forces become even more dangerous when they insist that their purposes and God's are the same.

4

The Church of Empire

The church of this country is not only indifferent to the wrongs of the slave, it actually takes sides with the oppressors.
—Frederick Douglass[1]

Douglass's words weren't directed at a particular church, but they could have been. No church in the United States of America compares to the Episcopal Church for longevity and depth of alliance with colonial, imperial power. For much of America's history, starting when we were but a group of British colonies and continuing well into the twentieth and twenty-first centuries, this particular branch of the Christian fold has energetically cooperated with, provided theological cover and blessing for, and received wealth and privilege from systems of colonization and White domination.

As an Episcopal priest, I call this church my home, but you don't have to be Episcopalian or even necessarily Christian to have a stake in the story that follows. It is one church's account of complicity with systems of self-centrism, exploitation, and subjugation—the

53

same systems that, in the end, not only wound the oppressed but also destroy the soul of the oppressor and separate us from being God's community of love. In the next chapter, we will also hear the stories of faithful people who refused to cling to privilege, moved with Jesus to the underside of empire, and in the process charted a path toward resistance, hope, and beloved community. But those stories live in a context—the context of privilege and White supremacy.

In 2017 the Episcopal Church pledged a long-term commitment to becoming beloved community (learn more at www.episcopalchurch .org/beloved-community). In order to fulfill that promise, this church and others like it will need to investigate our unique role in sustaining the nightmare too many of the children of God have suffered with the blessing and cooperation of dominant American Christianity. That honest reckoning will surely crack us open even further. Perhaps it will also lead to repentance, wisdom, and new life.

Walking the *Via Media* or Compromising the Gospel?

The Episcopal Church today is a global church of nearly two million whose reach extends across fifty states, most U.S. territories, and into an additional sixteen nations in Latin America, Europe, and Asia, but we didn't start that way. We were ourselves born as an extension of the British empire. As such, we have spent our entire life navigating competing vocations: on the one hand, the call to form followers of Jesus; on the other hand, the call to make good subjects of the crown and empire. When the monarch is also the legal head of your church and (for a time) your livelihood is sustained by the state, you can imagine which way you'll generally swing.

The die was cast from the church's foundation. Schoolchildren know the story of Henry VIII, the king of England who wanted a divorce and, when the pope refused to grant it, broke from the Roman Catholic Church in 1533. No doubt the king sought to remarry and make a male heir, but, more than that, he sought control over his realm. The church held vast power in the fifteenth century: power over finances, vast lands, and related holdings; power over laws and policies; and power over the hearts and minds of the people. The Holy Roman Catholic Church and the pope inherited much of the authority of the Holy Roman Empire, and they often exercised it on behalf of the Spanish and French. If Henry was to rule England, he needed to divorce the church in England from Rome.

That's not to say the birth of the Church of England was without theological merit, or that Thomas Cranmer, first Archbishop of Canterbury and spiritual architect of the new Church of England, was simply a pawn of the king. Cranmer instituted pivotal reforms like translating the liturgy into English and creating a Book of Common Prayer that empowered people to pray and learn on their own. But those reforms took place within the overarching commitment of church to crown and country. Queen Elizabeth I asserted that priority under no uncertain terms in the mid-sixteenth century. With what's known as the Elizabethan Settlement, she told warring Catholics and Protestants they could keep their doctrines and personal beliefs, as long as there was uniform use of the Prayer Book and peace in the realm.[2]

Wherever the British crown sent explorers, the Church of England was an essential instrument for assimilating colonized peoples to imperial culture. Just one hundred years ago, 85 percent of the earth was under European colonial rule, much of it English.[3] In these places, ordinations featured a vow to obey the king or queen who was, after all, the church's head. Clergy and buildings were controlled by the state and served its purposes. Prayers in the 1662 English Book of Common Prayer—truly the guide for common prayer throughout the realm—urged the faithful to be "sober," to tend their "duty," and to lead a "quiet and peaceable life."[4] It was the dream of the rulers, superimposed on liturgy.

Americans gained independence in 1776. While church leaders hurried to found a Protestant Episcopal Church for America and to erase vows to obey the monarch and other elements that simply did not match our new, more democratic principles, they kept much of the vaunted prayer language and biddings for sobriety, proper order, and quiet. These were exactly the socially controlled virtues and behaviors the new state needed the church to instill in its members.

It helped that the leaders of American government and mercantilism were often the ones in the pews. As Dwight Zscheile explains:

> Given that the church was led by the wealthy colonial elite (who controlled the vestries), this served the purpose of encouraging good order and decorum in the colonies. The Anglican Church in America went from being the officially established church to the church of the establishment as it remained favored by many of the socioeconomic elite. . . . In the words of Ian Douglas, the Episcopal Church saw itself as "a chosen people among an elect nation."[5]

To this day, our prayer language often assumes Episcopalians are the elite who control the levers of power and affiliate with the majority, dominant culture. One might rightly ask whether our prayers have shaped us into a community that comes to church seeking the succor, peace, and stability of empire's beneficiaries.

Again, this is true for the Episcopal Church but also for many other churches born of colonial and imperial rule, especially those linked to the Church of England. The Lambeth Conference—the roughly every-ten-years' gathering of bishops from the entire Anglican Communion—has remarked on these tendencies.

> [W]hen Anglicanism was exported to other continents, it came not only with the "Englishness" of certain styles of clothing, music and worship, but with certain assumptions about who made decisions, who had authority in social life, who had ultimate control in economic affairs, markets, production, land ownership. The dominance of the English style . . . could be seen as a reflection of the plain facts of political and economic dominance.[6]

Colonizers presented their own clothing, music, language, and bearing to conquered peoples as superior and preferred. They also had the political and economic power to force those preferences on everyone else.

This is a good time to note that Anglicanism contains a brilliant antidote to its own bent toward domination and uniformity: the ver- nacular principle. A staple among reformers, this principle maintains that worship and faith expressions should honor and rise from the people's language and culture. Thanks to the vernacular principle, English speakers can worship in English (a genuine innovation in the 1500s), Black Anglicans can incorporate gospel music, and Indigenous Episcopalians can hold leadership meetings using Native customs.

Anglicanism can and should always balance the ancient and the contemporary, the catholic and the vernacular. We call this middle way the *via media*, and it allows us to rejoice in having unity without uniformity, just as the early church did on that first multilingual, Spirit-filled Pentecost Sunday. We can flex and bend without break- ing. We can form citizens of the kingdom of God who bear peace, justice, and truth in the nations where we're planted. At times, we've lived into that fullness, but it has usually required vigorous swimming upstream. The current of empire and self-centrism is just that strong.

Anglican Blessing, Indigenous Curse

Our story has more often resembled that of Jamestown, Virginia, the first permanent English settlement in the Americas. When King James granted the Virginia Company's original charter in 1606, he prioritized spreading Christianity to the peoples of the new (to them) world. Men setting sail for Virginia first took an oath of allegiance to the king and the Church of England, disavowing any belief in the authority of the pope.[7]

One of the first structures built at Jamestown was a crude wor- ship space. Settlers stretched a sail among the tree branches and made benches from tree trunks. The altar was a log nailed horizontally between two trees. To instill discipline, men were sometimes required to attend church as much as fourteen times a week.[8] Anglican faith was at the center of the Jamestown enterprise.

The mostly English settlers at Jamestown weren't ready for the challenge of life in the swampy wilderness. John Smith, one of the Virginia Company's leaders, is usually credited with teaching those first settlers to farm and work. Roxanne Dunbar-Ortiz sets forth a different story from original sources.[9] In truth, the Jamestown Settlement was utterly dependent on the Powhatan Confederacy, a group of thirty tribal communities who had thriving villages and economies across the newly settled land. They provided for the English newcomers in exchange for peace. But when a drought struck and the Powhatan could not provide for both their own peoples and the settlers, John Smith threatened to make war and target Indigenous women and children. The Powhatan leader, Wahunsonacock, begged on behalf of his peoples:

> Why should you take by force that from us which you can have by love? Why should you destroy us, who have provided you with food? What can you get by war? . . . What is the cause of your jealousy? You see us unarmed, and willing to supply your wants, if you will come in a friendly manner, and not with swords and guns, as to invade an enemy.[10]

Their plea fell on unresponsive ears. Smith kept his promise and declared war against the Powhatan Confederacy in August 1609. His goal: annihilation.

British settlers employed this tactic in many of their encounters with Native peoples. In most cases, the British were evenly matched against their Indigenous opponents, and quite often they were actually outnumbered and outmaneuvered. Faced with little hope for a fair victory, the British took to what John Grenier describes as "extravagant violence."[11] They used extreme measures against civilians, women, elders, and children, seeking not only to defeat or even humiliate but to annihilate their enemies.

Look closely at this blood-filled scene, at White settlers collecting the heads of Indigenous women and children and receiving tribute from the British commanders. Look to the leaders and governors like John Smith who made the call to enact irregular warfare, theft, and genocide. You will find behind them the Church of England. As Dunbar-Ortiz explains, "When descendants of the settler class, overwhelmingly Presbyterian or otherwise Calvinist Protestant, were accepted into the ruling class, they usually became Episcopalians, members of an elite church linked to the state Church of England."[12] Starting in the 1600s and continuing to present day, America's leaders have visited unimaginable terror and betrayal upon Indigenous peoples, often with the tacit blessing or acquiescence of the Episcopal Church.

Triangle of Terror

The church also blessed every component of the global slave trade. Today, Anglican and Episcopal church leaders in Liverpool, Ghana, and Virginia are reckoning with their collective complicity in this dread chapter of human history. The three areas were once intimately connected in the Triangular Trade, a venture that involved building, stocking, and sending English ships from Liverpool; trading and purchasing captured Africans in Ghana; and sailing to the Americas, including Virginia, where Africans were sold into slavery and forced to work to provide cotton, sugar, and other commodities that returned enormous wealth and resources to England.

Liverpool was the origin and terminus for the trade, a role that earned it the moniker "European Capital of the Transatlantic Slave Trade." I visited the city in 2019 with a group of reconciliation leaders from Ghana and Virginia.[13] Together we learned about the English variety of slavery and how it differed from other forms around the world. The Roman Catholic Spanish and Portuguese enslaved, degraded, and violated people, as the Romans and other groups had done for millennia, but underneath each system was a fundamental recognition that these were human beings. Among the English, Ariela Gross observes, "For the first time in history, one category of humanity was ruled out of the 'human race' and into a separate subgroup that was to remain enslaved for generations in perpetuity."[14] Those subhumans were captured Africans.

I witnessed the Ghanaian leg of the triangle during a visit in 2017, when I retraced my African ancestors' steps from the interior communities across hundreds of miles to the Cape Coast slave fort.[15] As many as twelve million stolen Africans were shipped to the Americas from forts like this one. Just across the street from Cape Coast Castle, the Church of England's cathedral rises in majesty.

All of which brings us to Virginia once more. Nicknamed "Old Dominion," Virginia stood proudly at the center of English colonial life and the American slavocracy. As the wealthiest and most privileged church in America, and the direct descendant of the Church of England, the Episcopal Church was an active supporter of slavery and the broader system of White domination and supremacy.

Prior to the Revolutionary War, Anglicanism was the established church in the prosperous colonies of Virginia and New York, and the de facto state church across most of the South. As Harold Lewis explains in his landmark book *Yet with a Steady Beat: The African-American Struggle for Recognition in the Episcopal Church,* colonial powers provided clergy with land grants and collected a tax (called a tithe) that supported the church. When state leaders passed law after law codifying and strengthening slavery, the church said nothing. Its hands—and its tongue—were tied.[16]

In the decades leading up to the Civil War, the Presbyterian, Methodist, and Baptist churches publicly struggled and waged internal battle over the institution of slavery. During the same period, Pope Gregory XVI declared it unconscionable to enslave, persecute, or otherwise exploit "Indians, Negroes or other classes of men." In England, Anglicans were at the forefront of the abolitionist movement. In other words, there was a growing global Christian consensus against slavery, and even the other Euro-tribal churches in America were edging toward it.

Of all the churches in America, the Episcopal Church was arguably the most willing to continue accommodating slaveholders, traders, and upper-class racists, and the least likely to welcome the equal and full participation of Black people, slave or free. James Birney's 1842 classic, *The American Churches*, studied the role each of the denominational families played in supporting slavery. He made this case against the Episcopal Church:

> Its congregations are mostly in the cities and towns, and they generally consist of persons in the wealthier classes of society. This, together with the smallness of its numbers and the authority of the Bishops, has prevented it from being much agitated with the anti-slavery question. . . . Although apparently desirous of keeping clear of all connection with the anti-slavery movement, the Episcopalians have not failed when a suitable opportunity presented itself, to throw their influence against it.[17]

Across the Atlantic, Bishop William Wilberforce of Oxford looked with shame at his American cousins. He wrote: "[The Episcopal Church] raises no voice against the predominant evil [of slavery]; she palliates it in theory; and in practice she shares in it."[18] Far from decrying or even struggling over the slavery question, Episcopalians largely supported and shared in slavery's spoils while the world watched in dismay.

The Church of Southern Gentry

Slavery was essential to America's growing economic might, and especially in the South, that wealth and power flowed freely into the Episcopal Church. Walter Posey notes: "Nearly all of the Southern bishops owned slaves, either by inheritance or purchase. . . . When his wife had the option of inheriting money or four hundred slaves, Bishop Polk of Louisiana encouraged her to take the slaves, as he thought thereby he could function better in his state as a man of influence."[19]

For centuries, the ruling classes of the South had two things in common: the Episcopal Church and slavery. Elisabeth Evans Wray points out that the church could count among its members "the great majority of the landed slave-owning aristocracy of Virginia."[20] Southern slaveholders were encouraged to use tools like the catechism written by Virginia Bishop William Meade especially for slaves. It read, in part:

> Q. "What is the duty of servants?"
> A. "To be obedient to their masters in singleness of heart, as unto Christ not with eye service, as men pleasers, but as the servants of Christ; doing service as to the Lord and not men."
>
> Q. "What directions are given servants?"
> A. "Servants, obey in all things your masters according to the flesh; not with eye service as men pleasers, but in singleness of heart, fearing God."[21]

Meade was one of many Episcopal Southern bishops who defended and supported not only slavery but the broader dream of America as an exceptional nation that would represent the superiority of White, Anglo-Saxon civilization to the world. Just before the Civil War, a group of these bishops came together to establish the University of the South, a city literally perched on a hill (in this case, the mountains of East Tennessee). The university's Roberson Project on Slavery, Race, and Reconciliation has uncovered proof of the founders' White supremacist intentions. For instance, the university's original plans featured a School of Ethnology and Universal Geography, a field that studied how each geographic region was tied to a single race, and how each of those races were arranged in a divine order, with light-skinned Europeans and their descendants at the top and Africans and dark-skinned "savages" at the bottom. As the Roberson Project discovered, "The founders' and trustees' plan was to make the University of the South a recognized center for the study of race and thereby a sturdy ideological pillar of a civilization based on enslavement of people of African descent."[22]

In these ways and so many more, the Southern Episcopal Church itself served as one of the strongest pillars upholding a society founded on White supremacy, a self-centric vision in direct opposition to the reign of God.

The Northern Stake

The Northern church was arguably as invested in slavery as its Southern counterpart. Filmmaker Katrina Browne broke the relative silence about Northern Episcopal complicity with her 2008 documentary *Traces of the Trade: A Story from the Deep North*. The award-winning film followed members of her Rhode Island-based family as they reckoned with the Triangular Trade and their ancestor James DeWolf, an Episcopalian and the most prosperous slave trader in U.S. history.

As eye-opening as *Traces* was, the narrative could have been rooted in almost any state in the Northeast. Slavery was part and parcel of life in New York City, a stronghold for the Episcopal Church. Diocesan leadership stoppered their ears to protest against the city's slave trade, possibly because several landmark Episcopal churches were built and maintained with the labor of slaves and funds garnered via the slave trade.[23]

In Philadelphia, Episcopalians point with pride to St. Thomas Episcopal Church, the denomination's first Black church, founded by its first Black priest, Father Absalom Jones. We often skirt the fact that Pennsylvania denied St. Thomas a seat in its diocesan convention. At the time, opposition leaders said "the color, and physical and social condition and education of the blacks, render them unfit to participate in legislative bodies."[24] The Diocese of New York made the same case against the admission of St. Philip's Episcopal in Harlem, the second Black Episcopal church in America. It took St. Philip's eight years and tireless lobbying by Black leaders and their White allies to gain a seat.

Popular culture paints a picture of antebellum America as starkly divided, with Northern and Southern institutions battling on opposite sides of the conflict. No such wall existed in the Episcopal Church, where class solidarity often overruled regional affinities. As Gardiner "Tuck" Shattuck observes, "Friendships formed at schools and at summer resorts in the North . . . continued to unite bishops and leading clergy across sectional lines."[25]

There may be no better example of those binding ties than Bishop John Henry Hopkins. He led the Diocese of Vermont, but his family and church connections ran deep across the South. Two of his sons worked in the dioceses of Missouri and Louisiana, and, in 1859, the Southern bishops asked him to draw up plans for their proposed University of the South.[26] Later, on January 13, 1865, as the senior bishop in the House of Bishops, Hopkins took on the mantle of presiding bishop of the Episcopal Church.

On several occasions, colleagues prevailed upon Hopkins to write about slavery and Christianity. His early pamphlets outlined the scriptural case for slavery but allowed for a moral argument against enslaving fellow human beings.[27] As the Civil War loomed, and presumably as his friends down South grew more strident in their pleas, Hopkins shifted firmly into the pro-slavery camp and published "The Bible View of Slavery," one of the definitive texts on slavery and scripture. In it, he wrote:

> The slavery of the Negro race, as maintained in the Southern States, appears to me fully authorized both in the Old and the New Testament which, as the written Word of God, afford the only infallible standard of moral rights and obligations. That very slavery, in my humble judgment, has raised the Negro incomparably higher in the scale of humanity, and seems, in fact, to be the only instrumentality through which the heathen posterity of Canaan have been raised at all.[28]

During the Civil War, when Southern bishops pulled away to form their own Confederate church, Hopkins continued to have their names called at every vote in the House of Bishops. After the end of the war, as presiding bishop, Hopkins helped to reunite the Southern and Northern bishops. Again, it is important to note the friction in the

House was less over slavery and more over the rupture of their unity. The majority of Episcopal bishops and the church's top clergy and lay leaders consistently supported slavery and the presumption of White superiority, as we see in the story of Reverend George Freeman.

In 1836, Freeman was rector of Christ Church in Raleigh, North Carolina, and preached a series of sermons on slavery. He declared that slavery "was agreeable to the order of Divine Providence" and went on to insist that "no man, without a new revelation from heaven, was entitled to pronounce it wrong."[29] His bishop, Levi Silliman Ives, was present and approved of Freeman's message so wholeheartedly he arranged with other slaveholders to publish and circulate it as a pamphlet.

At the time, pro-slavery forces couldn't rely on many thoughtful Christian voices, so politicians tended to advance mostly economic arguments for slavery. When the Episcopal Church published these pamphlets, it threw out a lifeline, and slavery's supporters grabbed on tight. With their gratitude, Freeman's name and fame spread across the nation.[30]

Only eight years later, in 1844, the General Convention of the Episcopal Church met in Philadelphia to select a missionary bishop for Arkansas, Texas, and Indian Territory. America's political leaders argued about how or whether to support the practice of slavery in these territories. Episcopalians were not torn. The House of Bishops nominated, and the clergy and lay deputies confirmed, the Right Reverend George Freeman as bishop to carry the gospel and grow Episcopal ministry in this mission field. Yet again, the Episcopal Church willfully blessed and sanctioned the workings of empire, just as the church had been formed to do from its birth.

Moving against Movements

Given such history, it makes perfect sense that Black people fled the Episcopal Church after emancipation. This mass exodus genuinely baffled White Episcopal leaders, many of whom watched with jealousy and resentment as other denominations welcomed Black Christians baptized and even catechized by the Episcopal Church. Was it our worship style? Was it the ecclesiastical hierarchy? More than anything else, Black leaders cried out for the one thing the Episcopal Church would not grant: respect as fellow children of God.

In the limited cases where the Episcopal Church allowed Black congregations, it generally assigned them White clergy. Even when Black clergy served, they did so under humiliating conditions. Anna Julia Cooper mourned this state of affairs in 1892:

> A colored priest of my acquaintance recently related to me, with tears in his eyes, how his reverend Father in God, the Bishop who had ordained him, had met him on the train on his way to the diocesan convention and warned him, not unkindly, not to take a seat in the body of the convention with the White clergy. To avoid disturbance of their godly placidity he would of course please sit back and somewhat apart.[31]

I find it telling that the bishop did not argue the case for Black inferiority or unfitness (though I expect these were a given). The great danger in welcoming a Black priest was disturbing the placidity and peace of the church proceedings. For a community founded on and charged with maintaining the established social order, a break with decorum and uniformity would be the highest violation. No doubt the bishop and other church leaders could reassure themselves they were not motivated by racism, but simply by a need to preserve good order.

Indeed, police officers were often enlisted to oversee Black worshipers and to ensure "good order and propriety."[32] Black congregations were forced to accept the leadership of White vestries drawn from other parishes (this practice continued into the 1960s).[33] In several Southern communities, White Episcopalians tried to bar Black people from worship.[34] Once bishops began to enforce canons that forbade segregation, some Whites simply left. Stories from the 1930s and 1940s tell of churches that advertised the day's lynchings in their Sunday bulletins, so that members could take a picnic basket and watch after worship.[35] The racial violence of the culture found a comfortable home in some of our churches.

As Americans began to wrap their minds and hearts around civil rights, with Christians leading the way, Episcopalians were sometimes at the forefront but more likely to be the hesitant, late adopters. When the wider church finally began to shift, scholars like John Kater say it did so partly to maintain the church's role at the center of American established order.[36] If the nation needed peace, order, and reassurance as it moved through social tumult, the Episcopal Church would help to provide it, as the church of the powerful had since its founding.

To this day, the church's story in relation to communities on the underside of empire is often marked by ambivalence. The Right Reverend John Burgess was the first Black Episcopalian to serve as a diocesan bishop, which meant he saw the inside workings more clearly than almost anyone. Burgess argued for inclusivity and integration across the church, only to see Black churches and members consistently stripped of their power and identity. He noticed that "black parishioners in many such cases either found a cool welcome or discovered that they became second-class citizens in the merged parish."[37]

Though their stories may be more recent, Latinx and Asian peoples in the Episcopal Church have also often met a chilly welcome, if not outright disdain. The House of Bishops Theology Committee's 2020 paper on White supremacy takes care to highlight the church's history of Asian mission. As anti-Asian, exclusionary policies ramped up from the 1880s to the 1940s, the church was generally silent.[38] Some churches out West had developed strong relationships with Chinese laborers. When one such church burned down in 1875, and Congress passed the Chinese Exclusion Act of 1882, the Diocese opted to close the church rather than protect its Asian members.

The pattern continued from 1910 into the 1940s, when the Episcopal Church launched no new Asian missions. (Japanese Episcopalians who were forced into internment in the 1940s returned and rebuilt on their own.) The Theology Committee paper notes: "An apathetic silence was the Church's response to the plight of its Asian communities, both in the local dioceses and in the Episcopal Church nationwide."[39]

Latinx Episcopalians are among the fastest-growing group in the church, but leaders have no illusions about the church's full embrace of Latinx people and culture. Juan Oliver serves as the custodian of the Book of Common Prayer and regularly witnesses the church's resistance to non-White culture and power. "The interpersonal dynamics of 'inclusion' always involve an 'includer' and an 'included,'" he says. "In the Episcopal Church, Latinos [what we call ourselves] are always being invited, included and ministered to. We never get to do anything for ourselves. This usually means that we are welcome guests in someone else's house."[40]

This is precisely the sort of dynamic one expects in a church built on the foundations of colonialism, empire, and self-centrism. The primary mode for relationship with non-Whites and other outsiders would be welcome and charity; sharing belovedness and mutuality within the reign of God would require a whole other level of imagination.

America's Christian Elite

While I have focused on White supremacy as the arena where the Episcopal Church plays out its alliance with systems of empire, establishment, and domination, I cannot close this chapter without acknowledging the reality of classism and elitism. If America's founders believed they were establishing a superior, White city on a hill, the Episcopal Church stood at the city's pinnacle.

Once upon a time, the Episcopal Church could claim the lion's share of presidents and members of Congress—stunning when you consider the church's modest numbers. While those halls of power have diversified over the last century, many studies continue to show a disproportionate percentage of leaders in government, business, and education identify as Episcopalian or were shaped by Episcopal institutions.[41]

Class and social influence have long been a given for the Episcopal Church, as Kit and Fredrica Konolige argue in their 1978 social history, *The Power of Their Glory: America's Ruling Class: The Episcopalians.* The couple studied the overwhelming financial, intellectual, and social power that members of the Episcopal Church hold, and it is worth noting how those figures hold over time. In 1976, they report, 48 percent of Episcopalians were top earners (making more than $20,000 a year), while only 21 percent of the general American population made that much. By 2014, 36 percent of Episcopalians were in that top category (more than $100,000)—a higher proportion of wealthy people than any other Christian group, and far more than the 18 percent of the total population who make that much.[42]

Similarly, in 1976, about 45 percent of Episcopalians had gone to college, compared with 29 percent of all Americans. By 2014, 56 percent of Episcopalians had finished college or graduate school; while only 27 percent of the general population had obtained those levels of education. In other words, over a period when financial and educational gains decreased for most Americans, members of the Episcopal Church remained comfortably, consistently on top.

Upon assembling mountains of evidence, the Konoliges conclude that America's aristocracy could more accurately be called "Episcocrats."[43]

> What has made them so important to the country is that their set of attitudes and mores, fertilized by a distinctly Anglophiliac and Episcopal atmosphere of feeling, has been adopted by non-Episcopalians as the standard for upper-class conduct (in law, government and business). The influence of the distinctly Episcopalian institutions—the prep schools, the men's colleges, and the metropolitan clubs—can hardly be overstated.[44]

We have long been the church of the slaveholders, industrialists, and the owning and managing classes—in short, the church allied with power and control. The Konoliges called it as they saw it.

I realize words like "upper class," "elite," and "empire" are touchy in America, and the title "Episcocrat" might send some readers running. If you reflect on the period after the Revolutionary War, our affiliation with particular cultural and socio-economic groups makes more sense. Toward the end of the eighteenth century, the English ruling class had fled, and Anglo-Saxon–identified revolutionaries and founders quickly filled the vacuum and became institution-builders. The Episcopal Church was the natural church to contain and preserve the culture, values, and aesthetic of this Anglo-Saxon, American elite. If you wanted access to those elite circles, or simply gravitated toward their sober and orderly culture, the Episcopal Church was the ideal church home.

Today, the prominence of a defined Episcopal ruling class has faded, as has our cache as the church of American establishment. Ongoing decline and disruption have humbled and opened us to embracing more of the vernacular, the local and multicolored expressions in our surrounding communities. And yet, especially when it comes to liturgy, education, and social standing, Episcopalians continue to resonate with elite culture and Whiteness. We still bear the marks of the empire we were created to serve.

5

Shards of Light

Those who are cowards will ask, "Is it safe?"
Those who are political will ask, "Is it expedient?"
Those who are vain will ask, "Is it popular?"
But those who have a conscience will ask, "Is it right?"
                                                    —Paul Washington[1]

For too many years and in too many ways, the churches of the American White majority have served as chaplains to empire and allied with colonizing, dominating, fundamentally self-centric cultures and systems. The truth of it is almost enough to make you despair.

Don't.

Because every now and then, a crack has formed. Light has broken through. Individual people and entire church leadership bodies have contradicted their shameful history and cast their lot with the underside. In the mold of Jesus in Philippians 2, they did not cling to privilege but surrendered it and laid power at the service of the very groups the church had actively dominated and rejected. They made sacrificial, sometimes painful choices for the sake of love.

So yes, we need to hear the stories of the church's failure and complicity in order to comprehend the long road to beloved community. We also need to know about the grace-filled moments when Christians have turned from empire to follow Jesus. Just as it was helpful to examine the Episcopal Church and its capitulation to empire, it is worthwhile now to dwell with the witness of Episcopalians who resisted and remained steadfast in the way of Jesus. None of them is perfect. None is a "saint." Still, if there is any hope for new life in our current moment of chaos and opportunity, we may find it while listening deeply to ancestors and companions who turned away from empire, privilege, and self-centrism, recentered their lives on Jesus, and walked toward God's beloved community.

John Jay II: Risking All for His Friends

In 2019, the Diocese of New York approved a set of racial justice resolutions that had come before the convention on the eve of the Civil War. The man who offered that prophetic call some 160 years earlier was John Jay II.

The grandson of the first chief justice of the U.S. Supreme Court and the son of a judge (both known for their opposition to slavery), John Jay II pushed the boundaries and deepened his relationship with Black people, to the point that his fellow Episcopalians commented on his "negrophilism."[2]

Jay was born in New York City in 1817 and educated at the Muhlenberg Institute, a boys' school in Queens started by noted evangelical priest and critic of slavery Dr. William Augustus Muhlenberg. In 1834, when he was only seventeen and still studying at Columbia College, Jay helped found and then led the New York Young Men's Anti-Slavery Society. While other liberal-minded people argued the merits of colonization—that is, freeing Black people and promptly moving them to Africa—he firmly believed Black people belonged as citizens of the nation they had built.

That stance placed him at odds with his conservative Columbia professors and classmates, many of whom were the sons of New York's cotton-trading commercial families.[3] It also placed him at odds with his church. In 1839, fresh from legal studies, a twenty-two-year-old Jay posted this word, titled "Thoughts on the Duty of the Episcopal Church in Relation to Slavery," to his fellow Episcopalians:

> [The Episcopal Church] has not merely remained a mute and careless spectator of this great conflict of truth and justice with hypocrisy and cruelty, but her very priests and deacons may be seen ministering at the altar of slavery. . . . Her Northern clergy, with rare exceptions, whatever they may feel on the subject, rebuke it neither in public nor in private, and her periodicals, far from advancing the progress of abolition, at times oppose our societies, impliedly defending slavery, as not incompatible with Christianity, and occasionally withholding information useful to the cause of freedom.[4]

Jay admired leaders in the Church of England who leveraged their moral authority to pressure the British to outlaw the slave trade in 1807 and to free West Indian slaves in 1833. Why couldn't the Episcopal Church, a powerful force in the so-called land of the free, take a similar stand? Instead, he witnessed a church that fully complied with the racist order of the day.

Jay flung himself into reforming the church and laboring for justice. The same year he issued his "Thoughts" manifesto, he learned of the case of Alexander Crummell, a gifted young Black man seeking ordination in New York. Crummell was later regarded as one of the foremost Black scholars and churchmen of his century, but back in 1839 he was a member of St. Philip's Episcopal Church and an applicant to General Theological Seminary, the Episcopal training ground in New York. Though Crummell met all the criteria, the committee refused to admit him and instead offered him private instruction, so that he would not appear on General's student rolls and anger its Southern supporters.[5]

Jay immediately showed up at Crummell's door. Though they were strangers, Crummell later recalled, "He had heard of the rude and unjust treatment I had received, and came to tender his sympathy and succor."[6] Jay went on to sound the alarm in a letter to the *New York American*. In it, he said the church had "deliberately established a system of Caste" and lamented, "That Bishops should ever side with the oppressor is strange indeed."[7] In the end, Crummell attended Yale and then Cambridge University—with Jay's personal financial support and friendship—and was ordained in Massachusetts.

Jay also defended Crummell's sponsoring church, St. Philip's, against discrimination in the Diocese of New York. The church was founded in 1809 and supported by Trinity Church on Wall Street, but some of that institution's leaders fought to ensure no St. Philip's delegates were seated at the diocesan convention.[8] When Jay filed a resolution in 1845 to admit St. Philip's, a diocesan committee asserted that Black people were "socially degraded and improper associates for the class of persons who attend our Convention." It was one thing to allow the existence of a Black church, but another to allow Black people to join the councils and company of the rest of the church.

St. Philip's struggle lasted eight years, and Jay stayed by their side the whole time. At one point his own church, St. Matthew's in Bedford, grew uncomfortable with his radical stand and refused to send him to the convention as their delegate.[9] George DeGrasse, a member of St. Philip's vestry, once said of Jay: "You closed your ears to enticements of popularity and calmly chose the almost deserted pathway of philanthropy and freedom."[10]

Jay continued to file St. Philip's petition every year, and finally, in 1853, the convention voted overwhelmingly to recognize St. Philip's and to seat its delegates. Opponents seethed and spit at Jay. In his diary, Trinity vestry member George Templeton Strong wrote: "Another revolution. John Jay's annual motion carried at last, and the nigger delegation admitted into the Diocesan Convention. John Jay must be an unhappy, aching void . . ."[11]

Outside of church, as an attorney in private practice, Jay became New York's leading defender, often at no cost, of fugitive slaves seeking freedom in the state.[12] His peers in New York's polite society punished him for such alliances; it was likely the reason why he was exiled from the Union Club in 1851.

In 1859, Jay launched an almost one-man crusade to convince the Diocese of New York to oppose the city's still-robust participation in the slave trade. Episcopalians had long adjusted to the reality that their prosperity was tied to slavery and that the church should not interfere in their economic well-being. Jay couldn't abide such a moral compromise.

The first time he submitted the anti-slavery resolution to the church convention, he was met with booing and hissing in the convention and attacks in the press. Not one person seconded the motion. Even a fellow liberal shook his head at Jay's efforts and called him a "pertinacious and persistent friend of the negro" who unfortunately "always seemed to pick the wrong time to appear with the inevitable negro."[13]

The next year Jay presented a set of resolutions urging the bishop and clergy to write and preach against the illegal and immoral slave trade and urging laypeople in influential positions to do their part as well. Just as he prepared to speak, the chair allowed a motion to table the resolutions. Jay was stunned and silenced.

Later in the convention, he took the floor and—with the same vigor he must have brought to his defense of fugitive slaves—he laid out a fiery case arguing why the Episcopal Church in particular was obliged to speak and act to end the slave trade. He lifted up a critique from the *London Christian Observer*, whose authors observed with sadness: "Even the Episcopal Church then, it appears, is quite prepared not merely to justify men stealers, but to add the weight of its authority to their hideous cause."[14]

Jay suffered interruptions and shouts throughout the speech, but he cited the ancient African church fathers as his witnesses to the truth:

Go back to far antiquity and you have the voice of St. Cyprian writing to the Bishops of Numidia. "Both religion and humanity make it a duty for us to work for the deliverance of the captives. . . . It is Jesus Christ himself whom we ought to consider in our captive brothers. It is Him we should deliver from captivity, Him who hath delivered us from death."[15]

Jay did not live to see his church affirm the full humanity of Black people. He did not hear Bishop Andy Dietsche address the Diocese of New York's convention in 2019 and admit, "We have a great deal to answer for. We are complicit."[16] He did not see the diocese create a reparations fund of $1.1 million, which comprises 2.5 percent of its endowment. Yet Jay's sacrifice paved the way for healing, repair, and the in-breaking of God's reign in our day.

Vida Scudder: Companion of the Poor

There is nothing in Vida Scudder's background to suggest she would become a radical champion of the social gospel and a steadfast companion of Boston's poorest residents. She was born in 1861 and came of age during the rise of industrial expansion, robber barons, and urban slums. Though she grew up Congregational, Scudder chose at age fourteen to be confirmed an Episcopalian.

During this period, Episcopalians were shifting from our identification with the slavocracy and becoming the managing and owning class. In a social hierarchy supposedly ordained by God, the Episcopal Church presented itself as the keeper of the nation's unity, order, and traditions.

Women of Scudder's status were sheltered in life and educated at the best schools. Scudder earned both her bachelor's and master's degrees at Smith College. Even among those thoughtful peers, she was bored, restless, and frustrated. "We are all segregated in the prison of class," she wrote. "[O]ur culture is bound to remain tragically cramped and incomplete."[17]

Upon graduation, Scudder traveled to England and became one of only a few women admitted to study at Oxford. She sat in on social critic John Ruskin's final lectures and was captivated by his analysis of the emptiness and self-centeredness of contemporary culture, and his gospel-based vision of an egalitarian society. The young Scudder was struck with an "intolerable stabbing pain" and started to recognize the "plethora of privilege in which my lot had been cast."[18] She later wrote in *My Quest for Reality*: "I cannot shut myself away [in libraries] and study medieval legends while today men are perishing for the Bread of Life."[19] Her awakening had begun.

Following the example of other Ruskin students, Scudder joined the Salvation Army. No doubt the Army's sending-forth prayer resonated deeply in her newly cracked-open heart:

> While women weep, as they do now, I'll fight;
> while children go hungry, as they do now I'll fight;
> while men go to prison, in and out, in and out, as they do
>   now . . .
> I'll fight, I'll fight to the very end![20]

And fight she did. In partnership with social gospel leaders like Walter Rauschenbusch, she advanced beyond the Salvation Army's focus on individualism and developed a systemic analysis of poverty. She came to understand the forces of oppression and sin operating in society were like a "kingdom of evil," with capitalism at the heart of it all. She worked to ensure institutions—not just individuals—would repent and be converted.[21]

Scudder came home to Massachusetts to teach at Wellesley College, and she inspired students from several East Coast schools to form a College Settlements Association. The group established Denison House, a settlement house in Boston, and Scudder lived there throughout much of the year. Denison served as home base for several trade unions and provided as many as fifteen hundred people a week with employment assistance, English classes, child-care, and manual training.

She kept her connections to social elites in order to usher them into Denison House and help them to hear and heed the wisdom of the underside. With all her education and privilege, she had learned the solutions to social ills could be determined "only through the co-operation if not through the initiative of those suffering from them."[22] Following the lead of her poor neighbors, she struggled against sweatshops, child labor, and slum housing, and marched and spoke at strikes alongside workers.

Scudder's activism was deeply rooted in a vibrant relationship with God. She once wrote about what she understood to be the "Great Adventure of Faith": divesting oneself of privilege, in the footsteps of Jesus.

> [T]he distinctive contribution of religion to the modern crisis is to encourage its more prosperous disciples to ally themselves with the tendencies which will impoverish them and handicap their power. . . . It is spiritual suicide for the possessors of privileges to rest, until such privileges become the common lot. This truth is what the Church should hold relentlessly before men's eyes.[23]

Maybe her peers thought Scudder a traitor to her class. For her, the real loss—the "spiritual suicide"—would have been remaining identified with privilege and empire.

Scudder did more than write and talk about radical commitment. She joined forces with Episcopal women in the Society of Companions of the Holy Cross, a community devoted to social action and selfless intercessory prayer (prayer for others). Scudder was personally convinced this type of prayer "most perfectly unites our love for God and for our neighbor . . . and overcomes the last danger of spiritual self-culture."[24] Even in prayer, she was determined to center not on self but on God and neighbor.

Scudder devoted her life to driving comfortable Christians to release privilege and establishment, to embrace a very real and practical poverty, and to transform oppressive systems side by side with those who suffer most. Renunciation of privilege was not punishment.

She trusted Jesus, who promised that in losing our lives, we gain abundant life."

Jonathan Daniels: We Are Indelibly One

Like Scudder, Jonathan Daniels grew up Congregational and converted in college to the Episcopal Church. He would have been familiar with what Gibson Winter in 1961 called the "suburban captivity of the churches"[25]—a version of Protestant Christianity that thrived in relationship with suburban culture and insulated Christians from the world Jesus loved. This brand of dominant White American church focused on inner, personal, spiritual needs, and turned its back on cities bubbling with economic and racial tension.

In the 1950s and early 1960s, the majority of Episcopalians had little appetite for engaging the social struggles of the day. Arthur Lichtenberger was elected presiding bishop in 1959 and declared the church's mission should be transforming society. Yet on the ground, in actual congregations and dioceses—and even within the General Convention—Episcopalians often resisted integration and action. Bishops as a group tended to urge obedience to the law, regardless of what Lichtenberger preached.[26] Even when Lichtenberger and other bishops urged support for the 1954 Supreme Court decision that desegregated America's schools, local churches and dioceses organized and grew segregated schools where White children could avoid integration.[27]

At the end of 1959, John Morris and Cornelius "Neil" Tarplee gathered supporters to launch the Episcopal Society for Cultural and Racial Unity (ESCRU), a group that encouraged civil disobedience and kneel-ins. Several priests were jailed. At one trial, the judge reportedly quoted from the Book of Common Prayer and reminded his fellow Episcopalians of the call to "respectful obedience to the Civil Authority."[28] Social action like this was most un-Episcopal behavior.

It is fair to say the Episcopal Church was by and large neutral or even resistant to the emerging civil rights movement. On March 7,

1965, the tide shifted. By this time, Jonathan Daniels had graduated
from Virginia Military Institute and was preparing for priestly ordination at Episcopal Theological School in Cambridge, Massachusetts.
He joined ESCRU but also thought it best that outsiders avoid inter-
fering with the Southern struggle, as advised by Bishop Charles
Carpenter of Alabama.[29]

On March 7, 1965, Daniels and a group of seminarians gathered around the television to watch as police viciously attacked
peaceful demonstrators trying to cross the Edmund Pettus Bridge
in Montgomery, Alabama. The very next day, Martin Luther King
Jr. begged people of goodwill to come South and aid the nonviolent
struggle for justice. Daniels later reflected that he was surprised by
an internal voice whispering that *he* should go to Selma.[30] He shoved
the idea aside.

That night, he made his way to Evening Prayer. Together with his
peers and professors, he sang the *Magnificat*, Mary's song rejoicing
at God's activity through her and her son Jesus. That night, Mary's
prophecy pierced him like never before:

> My soul doth magnify the Lord,
>> and my spirit hath rejoiced in God my Savior.
>
> For he hath regarded
>> the lowliness of his handmaiden.
>
> For behold from henceforth
>> all generations shall call me blessed. . . .
>
> He hath showed strength with his arm;
>> he hath scattered the proud in the imagination of their
>> hearts.

Joining in the song of Jesus's mother Mary, Daniels wrote that he
was "peculiarly alert, suddenly straining toward the decisive, luminous, Spirit-filled 'moment'" . . .

> He hath put down the mighty from their seat,
>> and hath exalted the humble and meek.

> He hath filled the hungry with good things,
> and the rich he hath sent empty away.

Mary's revolutionary cry helped to turn Daniels's face toward Selma. A day later, he traveled to Selma with fellow seminarian Judy Upham. On Palm Sunday in 1965, they were part of a mixed-race group that dressed with care and respectfully attempted to attend St. Paul's Episcopal Church in Selma. He recalled: "We were startled from our vision by a member of the congregation entering the church as we did. His greeting was unmistakable: 'You g*d-d*mned scum . . .'"[31]

While his own Episcopal Church was less than welcoming, Daniels tentatively found the Black community and then fully embraced the young civil rights workers. One mother admitted she would not have allowed White people into her home even months before Daniels and Upham arrived. "Though saddened, we were grateful for her honesty and told her so," he wrote. "We also told her that though we would understand if she didn't believe us, we had begun to love her and her family deeply."[32]

He and Upham returned to Cambridge to finish the semester. By August 1965, they were back in Alabama. His family, seminary peers, and even some fellow justice seekers didn't understand the pull. Daniels could only explain it this way:

> [S]omething had happened to me in Selma, which meant I had to come back. I could not stand by in benevolent dispassion any longer without compromising everything I know and love and value. The imperative was too clear, the stakes too high, my own identity was called too nakedly into question. . . . I had been blinded by what I saw here (and elsewhere), and the road to Damascus led, for me, back here.[33]

The scales had fallen from his twenty-six-year-old eyes, and he could not pretend otherwise. Black lives were already on the line, and his life was now knit with theirs.

On August 14, Daniels and his friends were arrested at a demonstration and taken to jail in Hayneville, Alabama. The group of Black and White young people spent six days locked in small, overcrowded, summer-hot cells. Daniels kept spirits up by leading the group in prayer and song.

They were released on August 20 and a group of four made their way to a market to buy cold drinks. Deputy Sheriff Thomas Coleman was waiting for them with a shotgun. He attempted to shoot Ruby Sales, a Black teenager in the group. Daniels shoved her to the ground, and Coleman's bullet killed him. Coleman was later charged with manslaughter and claimed he was acting in self-defense. An all-White jury acquitted him.[34]

Jonathan Daniels was not the only Episcopalian to stand for justice. He was one of a few who surrendered privilege and took up the cross with suffering neighbors, because of the call to embody God's just reign and the conviction that God made us for beloved community. As he wrote to a friend a week before his death: "I began to know in my bones and sinews that I had been truly baptized into the Lord's death and resurrection . . . with them, the black men and white men, with all life, in him whose Name is above all names that the races and nations shout . . . we are indelibly and unspeakably one."[35]

Paul Washington: Power to All the People

Privilege and power come in myriad forms. Some people are called to renounce or subvert racial or class privilege. I am a Black woman, but I also hold the power that accrues to straight, educated clergy with economic means (though I grew up working class and carry that identity in my bones, too). People like me have the choice to ally with power, participate in domination systems, and reap the promised rewards.

Paul Washington was a Black priest in Philadelphia from 1954 to 1987, and he had many of the same options. Few would have faulted him if he clung to the safety and privilege his education and class background provided. It would have been triumph enough for a Black man born in Charleston, South Carolina, in 1921 to succeed at all.

For Washington, it was not enough. He had access to plum positions and power. Instead he crossed borders of class and privilege to join the Black Power movement and to honor poor and forgotten people, and he risked his ministry to guarantee women's rights in the church. Asked why he so often landed on the margins—and brought the church with him—he was known to say:

> Those who are cowards will ask, "Is it safe?"
> Those who are political will ask, "Is it expedient?"
> Those who are vain will ask, "Is it popular?"
> But those who have a conscience will ask, "Is it right?"[36]

Washington's father set a quiet but steadfast example that his son yearned to follow. The family wasn't upper class or light skinned, so they didn't occupy the highest rung on the Black social ladder. Theirs was a modest and dignified life, and Washington admired his father's belief that "it was a divine command that we respect everybody, both in the home and outside."[37]

His mother planted the seed for ordained ministry, but Washington never connected with the Baptist pastors of his youth. It wasn't until he heard a knock at the door and met Rev. Matthew Davis, the Episcopal chaplain at Lincoln University, that he found a minister in whom he could also see something of himself. Washington trained for priesthood at Philadelphia Divinity School, where he was the first Black student to live on campus. Except for a significant period when he and his wife, Christine, served as missionaries in Liberia, Philadelphia was his home.

The Church of the Advocate was already a respected center for urban ministry when Washington arrived in 1962. It was founded in 1900 as a middle- and working-class church without pew rents—a truly democratic move at a time when most Episcopal churches charged for pews and reserved the best spots for their most prestigious members. On the flip side, because the church was lower class, the diocesan powers insisted that members could not elect their own rector or handle financial and administrative decisions. Instead, the bishop designated a board of wealthy, outside trustees to manage the church's most important affairs. It was patronizing, but it was the only way diocesan leaders knew to do ministry with less privileged communities.[38]

In the 1940s, the dwindling White congregation at The Advocate received the members of a closed Black Episcopal church. By the time Washington came on the scene, The Advocate was a relatively integrated church with members who did good works but rarely rocked the boat. Looking beyond the sprawling building, he saw a neighborhood so riddled with crime and gangs that the police commissioner dubbed it "the Jungle." The bishop and the denominational-level leadership took a chance and invested in The Advocate and in Washington, hoping they would together create an example of vital Episcopal ministry in a troubled city.[39]

Washington took that call and ran with it . . . straight into the arms of suffering people. It broke his heart, he said, when he saw poor and needy people "treated like trash, blamed for being poor, dehumanized, and always kept waiting, waiting." He made up his mind early on that he would not participate in the dehumanization of his struggling neighbors. Instead, he would give himself away to them.

> I decided to give myself—my soul, my time, my resources—to everyone who came to see me. Every person was Christ: "Inasmuch as you have done it unto one of the least of these," Jesus said, "you have done it unto me." So I instructed my family: "When someone rings the doorbell and asks to see me, don't come to tell me and describe him—clean or dirty, drunk or sober, white or black. Just tell me, 'Someone is at the door to see you.'"[40]

That policy didn't sit well with the class-conscious teachers, doctors, city employees, and other professional people who made up the bulk of The Advocate's membership. He continued preaching and teaching at The Advocate as well as at White churches across the diocese and around the country, working to convince Episcopalians the church exists for just this kind of sacrificial, prophetic witness. The number of people in The Advocate's pews on Sunday mornings declined precipitously. The number who took part in community ministries and outreach climbed higher.[41] Washington took it as a sign they were on the right track.

Black leaders in Philadelphia grew to trust Washington more and more, even if he was an institution man. Student organizer John Churchville used The Advocate as his base for outreach with gangs. One day, he suggested The Advocate host a Black unity rally. Washington initially cringed: what business did the church have stirring such controversy? In his autobiography, Washington recalls how Churchville called him out:

> He said, "You are an Episcopalian. It is a church that represents the white establishment and racism in its most sophisticated but vicious fashion. You are going to have to make a choice, to fight for the liberation of our people and maybe get kicked out of this church, or you may reach a point where you have to leave."[42]

Washington quietly replied, "I'm going all the way." Then he did, leveraging his relationships in the church and in the city of Philadelphia, acting as translator from the streets to the institution and back again.

The Advocate hosted that Black unity rally. When national Black Power leaders asked him to serve as host in 1968 for a gathering of eight thousand people focused on Black consciousness and self-determination, he did. When the Black Panthers proposed Philadelphia as the base for their Revolutionary People's Constitutional Convention in 1970, he signed on. When Barry Hogan wanted to organize a peace gathering for Philadelphia's warring street gangs, he told Washington, "This is the only place where we can meet."[43]

And when the church discerned one of their own, a brilliant White organizer named Sue Hiatt, had a calling to the priesthood,

Washington said yes. In the face of prohibitions against women's ordination, knowing it might cost his priesthood, he acted as a supporter, listener, planner, and co-strategist. "At that time I knew only one thing: A black priest in an aided parish had disobeyed his bishop, the presiding bishop, and the General Convention in an action that was broadcast to the world. I was in trouble. . . . This was truly the lowest and perhaps the loneliest moment of my life."[44] But he kept going, because he also understood that the civil disobedience of the 1960s had prepared them for this act of ecclesiastical disobedience.[45]

On July 29, 1976, the Feast of Saints Mary and Martha, Washington and The Advocate made Episcopal history by hosting the irregular priestly ordinations of a group of women known as the Philadelphia Eleven. Three retired bishops performed the ordination. The critics raged. And the church took one step closer to the reign of God.

Reflecting on the ordinations at a tenth anniversary celebration, Washington said: "Today, with women laying their hands upon my head, I feel fully ordained," he once said. "Today, it was as though I discovered something I didn't have but did not know I'd missed, and it made me whole."[46] That dream of wholeness has stirred people in every age to move beyond self-centrism, beyond group, and beyond empire, in order to yoke their lives to God's dream. We have the same choice today.

———

I still imagine them: the woman with the cracked pieces of alabaster in her oil-drenched hands, and Jesus, full of resurrection light but also bearing the scars. Now they've got company. I see John Jay II, Vida Scudder, Jonathan Daniels, Paul Washington, and a whole cloud of witnesses: faithful people who risked and lost in the eyes of the world but gained a glimpse of God's beloved community. They can teach us now, if we are willing to listen and if we want beloved community more than peace, propriety, and protection. They are whispering and calling.

Now is the hour. Let it crack. Let it go.

6

Lose Your Life–Kenosis

Verily, I say unto you, Except a grain of wheat
fall into the ground and die, it abideth alone:
but if it die, it bringeth forth much fruit.

—Jesus in John 12:24, KJV

What do you do when the cracks form and truth creeps through the crevices? What do you do when you can see what's truly at the core of your nation, your church, yourself? Followers of Jesus before us have asked, struggled, found a way to hope, and then moved toward beloved community and true discipleship. Now we stand at our own inflection point. What do *we* do?

Again and again, in every gospel—and sometimes multiple times in the same gospel—Jesus offers a simple pattern for his disciples living in cracked-open times like these. In Matthew 10:39, he says: "If you try to save your life, you will lose it. But if you give it up for me, you will surely find it."[1] Mark 8:35 includes a twist: "For those who want to save their life will lose it, and those who lose their life for my sake, and *for the sake of the gospel*, will save it" (my emphasis). Some version of this message also shows up in Matthew 16:25, Luke 9:24 and 17:33, and John 12:25. What is Jesus telling us?

1. *Lose your life—Kenosis:* As individual Christians, faith communities, and institutions, we can practice kenosis and release our hold on false narratives, privileges, and self-centric structures built to serve empire, White supremacy, and the established order. Let die what needs to die, so that God's new creation can be born. Let the cracks form, let the jar break, so the oil can finally flow free.

2. *Gain real life—Solidarity:* Having opened and emptied, we practice solidarity. Move your body, your resources, your power, and your heart into place among the hurting people with whom Jesus already stands. That's when you gain abundant life, because that's when you begin to experience Jesus-shaped life.

3. *Walk in love—Discipleship:* In our daily life, we continue in Jesus's way of love. Commit to behaviors and relationships that nourish rather than dominate, share rather than hoard. If the self-centric way of empire prizes self and group above all else, and exploits and controls others for the prosperity and peace of those at the center, the way of love is its opposite. In this way, we constantly turn toward God, learn from Jesus, pray and worship and keep God at the center, offer our lives as blessing, go across borders to form beloved community, and rest together in the grace of God.

Jesus's way of healing love and communion is no mere dream. It is stunningly real and always available. In this chapter, we will explore more deeply what it means to follow him, first by losing your life.

Let It Die

In the summer of 2020, lost life was everywhere. The bodies of COVID-19 victims were stacked up in hastily dug trenches. Stores, businesses, and schools shuttered their doors, some never to open again. George Floyd, Breonna Taylor, Ahmaud Arbery, and Elijah McClain were all dead. Protesters, myself among them, risked their lives to hit the streets. Statues fell. Churches were humbled. The world's remaining superpower couldn't power its way out. The story of disruption, decentering, decline, and death was our shared story.

In the midst of it, I joined a call with two dear sister-friends, Kelly Brown Douglas and Winnie Varghese. The three of us share the experience of clergy women of color leading in the heart of the church of empire—Kelly as dean of Episcopal Divinity School and canon theologian at Washington National Cathedral, Winnie as priest for program and ministry coordination at Trinity Wall Street, me as a canon to the presiding bishop. Winnie shared these bubbling thoughts with us, offered here with her permission:

> I keep hearing Jesus saying, "Very truly, I tell you, unless a grain of wheat falls into the earth and dies, it remains just a single grain; but if it dies, it bears much fruit." And there's the King James: "Verily, I say unto you, Except a grain of wheat fall into the ground and die, it abideth alone: but if it die, it bringeth forth much fruit." It makes me think:
>
>> Let it die
>> the legacies of genocide and slavery that made America
>> the lies of conquest
>> the lies of pilgrims
>> the lies of White supremacy
>
>> Let it die
>> the deceit of redlining, Jim Crow, mass incarceration and . . .
>> from this fetid rotted death of so much possibility wasted
>> let us free the America that can be to emerge.

We let Winnie's wisdom resonate and reverberate deeply. Yes, death lay all around, too much of it unjust, preventable, and wrong.

But in the midst of unprecedented upheaval and disruption, could some things that needed to die also pass?

In particular, it was past time for the self-centric, sinful way of empire and domination to shake and topple, and with it White supremacy, misogyny, heterosexism, classism, elitism, ethnocentrism, and all the interlocking, well-crafted systems that secure rights, resources, and order for so few, to the detriment of so many. Our church had chaplained these systems, supporting and shoring them up whenever cracks emerged. This time, we could all choose to join up with God and push the cracks and crevices wider, so that truth could fully emerge and reality could profoundly shift.

But how? We should of course look to exemplars like the ones in the last chapter and reflect on how those faithful people cracked the jar and let the pieces fall so the healing oil could flow. They allowed God to crack their very lives open—and in the case of Daniels, he even lost his life—for the sake of love.

How do we personally move beyond talking and witnessing and embrace in our own lives and faith communities the disruption and decline that presage the inbreaking of God's reign? How do we let it go?

Kenosis Explained

This brings us full circle to a theological term you saw in chapter 2, "New Hope for Beloved Community." The word is *kenosis*, and it captures the self-emptying movement that privileged systems and the people who align with them must ultimately invite into our own lives. This mystery may be the deepest in Christianity or any spiritual tradition, so I'd like to revisit it more fully now.

The passage that best captures the essence of kenosis is Philippians 2:5–9. It is known as the "Kenotic Hymn" because it appears to be an early song that predates the gospels and Paul's letters. Imagine early Christians singing to teach one another about Jesus, long before anyone penned a word:

Let the same mind be in you that was in Christ Jesus,
who, though he was in the form of God,
    did not regard equality with God
    as something to be exploited,
but emptied himself,
    taking the form of a slave,
    being born in human likeness.
And being found in human form,
    he humbled himself
    and became obedient to the point of death—
    even death on a cross.
Therefore God also highly exalted him
    and gave him the name
    that is above every name . . .

Jesus's life on earth was a purely kenotic, downwardly mobile path. Jesus had the privilege of divinity, which meant he could remain separate from humanity, eternally dancing in the circle of the Trinity. He surrendered superiority and separateness in order to become equally human and divine, and extended his own life in order to welcome us into the life he shared with the Father and Spirit.

Once he embraced humanity, Jesus could have been a prince on a throne, holding power, riches, and every kind of privilege. Instead, he denied it. He let it go and joined us as a poor and vulnerable Jewish child in the backwater village of Nazareth, suffering under Roman imperial rule. Rather than work hard to elevate himself, he consorted with undesirables, tangled repeatedly with religious and civil authorities, and held up the picture of belovedness and shalom that he received from his Abba God. He consciously chose a path that assured suffering, humiliation, desolation, and finally death on a cross. In response, God lifted him up and gave him glory.

None of this was an accident or coincidence. Jesus entered as he did, where he did, doing what he did, because God needed us to finally comprehend the truth: God is not a sky king who heads an empire; God is the love that gives itself away for the sake of more love. Jesus could only communicate that point by standing outside the power structures and inviting disciples to join him and discover new life with him on the margins.

That's the path he opened up to his followers. In Luke 10, he instructs the seventy to go empty-handed and vulnerable into the world—the same way he approached the cross. Dwight Zscheile suggests that Jesus intended them to "practice dependence on the hospitality of the neighbor, as Israel was dependent on the hospitality of God in the desert. They were not to go as those in control."[2] Those who embrace kenosis and cross-shaped life constantly practice giving over control to God and allowing God's deepest yearning to become our own.

How I wish Christians and churches could internalize Jesus's total dedication to the kenotic path. It would make it easier for us to turn away from empire and domination and toward love. The kenotic path assumes we give something of ourselves away—some privilege, some piece of ego—in order to make more room for God and ultimately to honor, love, and sacrifice for the sake of the God we recognize in one another and in all of creation. It would help churches to embrace our cracked-open, uncertain, decentered state and give up some part of the institution's life, in order to gain more life with God.

What Kenosis Is Not

Let me be clear on one point before going much further: not all sacrifice and suffering is kenotic or redemptive. Some suffering, especially the pain others inflict without your choice, is wrong, and Jesus's followers should wholeheartedly work to prevent and alleviate it.

Certain groups have also historically borne an unfair, sacrificial burden for the sake of the whole, and I'm not willing to label that as redemptive or kenotic, either. For instance, Black, Latinx, and Asian women have been America's suffering servants for centuries, sacrificing our health and our own families in order to raise White children and clean up White homes and institutions. Likewise, American fields and factories have only ever worked because of immigrants who give their lives in the shadows, even as the nation's leaders posture and conspire to drive them out. And let us speak of the evil visited upon Indigenous peoples who were stripped of their land, traditions, languages, children, lives, and essentially disappeared by savage British and American colonizers. *These sacrifices are not kenosis.*

When someone forces suffering on you, or you're trying to satisfy the cravings of a punishing, bloodthirsty God, that's not kenosis. For millennia, penitents have scourged themselves raw or nailed others to the cross because they thought God required that kind of sacrifice. Thanks be to the God of liberation, we don't need to balance some cosmic scale in the hand of God: pain for pain, a death for a death. God does not desire sacrifice like this. The Psalmist and the prophet Isaiah together clarify what God wants most:

> For you have no delight in sacrifice;
>> if I were to give a burnt offering,
>> you would not be pleased.
> The sacrifice acceptable to God is a broken spirit;
>> a broken and contrite heart, O God,
>> you will not despise. (Psalm 51:16–17)

> Is not this the fast that I choose:
>> to loose the bonds of injustice,
>> to undo the thongs of the yoke,
> to let the oppressed go free,
>> and to break every yoke?
> Is it not to share your bread with the hungry,
>> and bring the homeless poor into your house;
> when you see the naked, to cover them,
>> and not to hide yourself from your own kin? (Isaiah
>> 58:6–7)

This fast, this sacrifice, this giving away for the sake of love—this is kenosis. When you take something you possess—your bread and power, your abilities and identities, your comfort and control, your treasured structures and even life itself—and release your attachment to it and make it useful to God's movement, you are practicing kenosis. It's what Vida Scudder did when she renounced class privilege, dwelled among poor women and children, and took to the streets by their side to struggle for justice. John Jay II did it every time he stood at the podium and suffered the scorn of his peers to speak God's truth about slavery. Paul Washington embraced it when he risked his own vocation to secure priesthood for women and to nudge the church toward becoming God's community of love.

In Jesus, God shows us what it looks like to be this vulnerable, humble, and self-giving. In him, we see one who did not run from the things that broke his heart, nor did he first calculate what he could gain from a situation. Jesus sought instead to give away his life, so he and others might flourish as God intends. And before you say, "Well, he was God; of course he did. What's that got to do with us?" note *how* Jesus did it. In the very first chapter of Mark, Jesus heads from Nazareth to be baptized by John in the River Jordan. Just as Jesus comes up from the waters, the heavens break open and the Holy Spirit descends on him like a dove. "And a voice came from heaven, 'You are my Son, the Beloved; with you I am well pleased" (Mark 1:10–11). Everything that follows is powered by the Spirit and by the love of God.

The same Spirit that Jesus received now rests on anyone who follows him. God invites us into a covenant, where by the power of the Spirit we can choose to allow our hearts to break, and then take the pieces—our lives, our goods, our love, and our privileges—and share it all like a broken loaf of communion bread.

Granted, this is a very non-American way of being. Think of the phrases that shape our national identity. We assert our "right" to "life, liberty, and the pursuit of happiness," which means we are free—and even expected—to organize our lives around our own individual desires. So much of our American story consists of groups of people protecting themselves and what's theirs, with a gun or a flag or the cloak of racial, class, or gender privilege.

Jesus's story is exactly the opposite. In this moment, as we reckon with the limits and consequences of self-centrism, domination systems, and the church's capitulation to empire, we could lean into the Jesus way. We could reclaim kenosis, or perhaps claim it for the first time.

Following Jesus, Taking Up the Cross

Jesus's embrace of the fullness of humanity and divinity was the definition of kenosis. He could have worked miracles that secured him fame and powerful friends; instead, he urged those he healed, "Don't tell anyone I did this." In his last days, when the authorities were closing in, Jesus could have simply skipped out of Jerusalem or at least kept a low profile. He could have asked God to spare him the suffering he knew was barreling his way. Jesus acknowledged his very real fear, looked death in the face, and just kept moving toward it.

Who does that? I don't, and neither do the vast majority of human beings, Christian or otherwise. Episcopal priest and contemplative Cynthia Bourgeault reflects on the limits of our human capacity for kenosis. "We can be magnanimous," she admits, "we can be friendly, we can be very spiritual, until the moment when our ass is on the line and then bang! It's backtrack fast." Jesus offers a different choice, the kenotic and self-giving choice. In the moment of truth, Bourgeault says, "you don't deter from love because of your fear for your own life . . . because love becomes the stronger principle."[3]

What if we believed and lived as if love is stronger than death, as if giving away our lives for one another actually restores and increases everyone else's life? What if we allowed the Holy Spirit to make possible a degree of loving and self-emptying that we, under our own individual power, could not possibly achieve? What if we trusted the wisdom of the earth, which teaches that a seed has to fall to the ground, crack open, and die—if it doesn't, it won't bear fruit. In Jesus's life, death, and resurrection, God seeks to reassure us that the countercultural, counterintuitive, perspective-shattering wisdom of kenosis is true.

The self-giving, kenotic love of Jesus becomes painfully, shockingly real on the cross. I doubt any part of the Jesus story or the whole Christian tradition lends itself more to misunderstanding and misinterpretation than the cross. His followers were unutterably confused as they witnessed the tragedy and humiliation of his death. Except for the women who stayed at the foot of the cross, the rest of his disciples averted their gaze from the shameful sight. We're not much more ready to accept it today.

Andrew Root explores our ambivalence about the cross and the idea of kenosis in his book *Faith Formation in a Secular Age*. According to Root, even the apostle Paul struggled to grasp this deepest mystery. "Paul had imagined that the cross was the smoking gun that eliminated this Jesus of Nazareth from messianic consideration,"[4] Root says. Surely a God who failed so spectacularly and publicly would be disqualified from divinity? How could Jesus be a savior when he couldn't or wouldn't even save himself?

In time, Paul learned that Jesus's self-giving way, especially on the cross, wasn't a departure from divinity. If anything, Root explains, it illustrated the true nature of divinity. "Paul sees that the cross is not the unavoidable discontinuity between God's being and Jesus's own. Rather, kenosis is the very shape of God's being. . . . The cross is not the elimination of Jesus's election—the end of his chosenness—but its sure legitimation."[5] God gives God's life away in love. When Jesus does the same, he doesn't merely succumb to God's will. He reveals God's very nature.

This is what Jesus meant when he said "those who want to save their life will lose it, and those who lose their life for my sake, and for the sake of the gospel, will save it." In other words, if you cease clinging to your individual survival and thriving and share your whole self for the sake of love, you will be embraced into God's life.

Does this mean every Christian should find an instrument of torture on which to impale themselves to make some dramatic point? Absolutely not. Following Jesus in a kenotic way does not result in self-aggrandizement, shining a spotlight on what "I" will do for "them."

Cross-shaped life moves from release and renunciation to the flourishing and beloved community that are the promises of the gospel.

Real Kenosis in Real Life

So what does it take for us to embrace cracking open, letting go, and self-giving, as individuals and also in the communities and systems we build and nurture? Buddhism and Christianity agree on the same teaching here: the practice of non-attachment.

When the resurrected Jesus greeted Mary at the tomb, she reached out to grab and keep him with her. He shook his head. "Do not hold onto me," he told her. "Go to my brothers and say to them, 'I am ascending . . . to my God and your God.'" (John 20:17). If she had clung to him, he couldn't ascend. And if he hadn't ascended, the life God holds for Jesus and welcomes all people into would not be possible. He had let go of his life. She had to let go of it, too.

One of my favorite practical sages on this topic is Pema Chödrön, an American woman and teacher of Tibetan Buddhism. She speaks often of *shenpa*, a Tibetan word usually translated as "attachment" but which she prefers to define as "getting hooked."[6] Chödrön says we've all been in uncertain situations where we feel an underlying insecurity and have to grasp onto something.[7] That grasping and holding onto resources, established order, narratives, people, privileges, and life itself is the urge just beneath all human aggression, craving, conflict, cruelty, oppression, and greed. The way through is not to detach, to stop caring, or somehow to exit the world. Instead, we must learn to experience life fully without clinging to it or getting hooked—without *shenpa*.

Let's return to Cynthia Bourgeault for help on this front. Through centering prayer—a contemplative form of prayer where you dwell silently with God and use a single word, phrase, or your breath to literally stay centered—she has learned to let go of thoughts and interruptions as they come. You don't bully or wrestle them to the ground. You notice the thoughts, nod to them, maybe even become curious about why they're rising at this moment, and then you let them pass as clouds moving through the sky. This practice transfers seamlessly into regular life, as Bourgeault demonstrates:

> [Recognize] when you are stuck in a position of insisting or clinging or identifying, or putting your need or will against a situation. . . . And it's simply a matter of letting go. It doesn't even mean renouncing, like pushing away; it's much closer to what the folks in Alcoholics Anonymous call "being willing to have it taken away." So it's going through life, situationally, with a nonpossessive attitude.[8]

The early community of Jesus's followers cultivated this non-clinging posture. At the first Council of Jerusalem, when the church's leaders struggled over whether new Christians needed to be circumcised, Peter and his cohort were expected to demand adherence to the law. Instead, God worked on his heart in a series of dreams. Peter walked into the gathering with new insight: "I truly understand that God shows no partiality, but in every nation anyone who fears him and does what is right is acceptable to him" (Acts 10:34–35).

Peter had gotten hooked on the temptation to close Christianity's borders and to hoard his group's special relationship with God. He learned the wideness of God's love and mercy, which allowed him to embrace a future that he and these new gentile followers of Jesus could forge together.

Cracking Open Consciousness

Any of us can cultivate this capacity for self-emptying and non-attachment and spread it to our faith communities and institutions. The first major step may be cracking open consciousness.

These days, people call this the process of "getting woke." Brazilian liberation teacher Paolo Freire had another name for it: *conscientizacao*. It is the Portuguese word for "conscientization," or the development of critical consciousness. He outlined the concept in his

1970 classic *Pedagogy of the Oppressed*, a text about learning from and walking with the poor as both they and the oppressor become free. Freire watched and facilitated the process of *conscientizacao*, and he reveled as he saw people "*emerge* from their *submersion* and acquire the ability to *intervene* in reality as it is unveiled."[9]

What does that journey look like? We begin with one kind of consciousness—call it uncritical. Things occur and we don't see the patterns or reasons operating in the background. For instance . . .

- Why, at age eighteen, interning for a local newspaper, was I making more money per hour than my mother, who had spent a decade as the assistant to a university senior administrator? The uncritical perspective says my work was just worth more.
- Why do unarmed Black people keep getting shot by the police? They must commit more crimes.
- Why are our churches declining? People don't care about God anymore.
- Why don't more people of color or young people attend our church? We just have different preferences.

Life is full of these quandaries. Systems of domination, empire, and established order depend on us not asking more questions, making more connections, or caring about each other's realities. But the day *may* come, when "[s]omething punctures complacency, and the Spirit moves into that gap to draw our attention to the fact that not all is as it should be."[10] In other words, there is a crack in the wall of uncritical consciousness. Then *conscientizacao* is possible.

Pastoral care and anti-racism leader Tammerie Day outlines four steps in this process of growing critical consciousness, or losing your life:

1. Attend to reality.
2. Let ourselves feel.
3. Discover alternatives.
4. Engage in critical analysis.

You can explore these steps in greater detail in the Reflection & Action Guide, but let's explore them briefly now . . .

Step 1: Attend to Reality

At this first stage, information or an experience penetrates and presents a contradiction to what we understood to be reality. It can unfold over time, or it can be startling, as when the world watched officer Derek Chauvin pressing his knee into George Floyd's neck until he died. Some people still cling to their original, closed picture of reality, mostly because they're terrified that if a crack forms, that crack might be the beginning of truly losing their life, or life as they've known it. People will do almost anything to *not* experience that loss, including closing themselves off from information that might crack the shell. H. A. Goodman explains it this way:

> If I put myself completely in the shoes of Trayvon Martin or Michael Brown, or even a black man denied the opportunity to board a taxi cab, I must accept the reality that my world and my America isn't their world and their America. . . . For many [White] citizens, . . . such empathy would lead to an emphasis on questioning the status quo, and doing so might also mean facing the prospect of our nation being less than exceptional.[11]

People will fight to defend a particular identity or story—be it personal or national—because their lives depend on it.

Jesus understood this struggle and spoke directly to his disciples' fear when he said: "I still have many things to say to you, but you cannot bear them now. When the Spirit of truth comes, he will guide you into all the truth; for he will not speak on his own, but will speak whatever he hears, and he will declare to you the things that are to come" (John 16:12–13). That process of truth telling takes time, but the lies and partial truths that prop up systems of oppression and self-centrism cannot last forever. Eventually, sustained by the grace and abiding love of God, we can attend to what is real. Read the books.

Listen to the stories. Watch a different news program. Ask the questions. Let the cracks form.

Step 2: Let Ourselves Feel

In a world on the verge of collapse, who doesn't want to turn off and not feel? But there's a cost to not feeling, too. Imagine if your house is on fire but you tell yourself it's not hot. That won't prevent the house from burning down, but it might just stop you from getting the help you need in time to make a difference.

Letting yourself feel is a step toward being fully, truly alive. It also opens you to an avalanche of difficult emotions, as Goodman warns:

> With empathy comes responsibility and culpability, self-reflection, sometimes guilt, oftentimes anger, and almost always a certain amount of regret. . . . Then there's the issue of simply surviving daily life without the burden of thinking about another American's pain; especially if like many Americans you struggle just to keep your marriage intact, or your kids in college, or simply live another day.[12]

I am more and more convinced that many supporters of oppressive, dominating systems are acting from a deep need to *not* feel. Maybe they've been taught their whole life to shove away emotions, and now they're scared that, if one gets through, the rest will overtake them. It can seem better to shove away negative emotions—and the truths attached to them—before they interfere and disrupt your life for good.

That's not the only choice. Psychology professor and therapist Sam Osherson has shepherded people through the process of being cracked open.[13] Underneath a lot of White reactivity around race—people report feeling angry, guilty, fearful, numb, overwhelmed—he detects a deep well of grief. His job is to help people to work with that sorrow. "Mourning takes resilience and grit," he says, "being able to acknowledge what has been lost (those cherished narratives and false beliefs) and to weave together a sense of oneself in a changed world."[14]

I know the idea of creating space for privileged people and institutions to mourn looks a lot like coddling and cooing over the oppressor's fragility. It doesn't have to be. If the goal is to join God in refashioning the church as beloved community, then a critical mass of people with power will have to stop denying reality and acknowledge how oppression and empire have compromised their humanity, too. I welcome that movement.

Step 3: Discover Alternatives

Once you're able to feel and the pain rocks but does not destroy you, the door to reality can fully open. When you are no longer afraid to feel the cracking open, you can look directly at the change or loss ahead. Instead of being defensive, you can become curious.

Curiosity is the secret superpower of resilient and flexible people. Curiosity allows you to wonder why that person believes what they believe, or why you were taught certain narratives that you are now coming to recognize as false. Faced with a situation where you have to let go of some resource, narrative, privilege, or element of reality, curious people can ask: "If I surrender this way of understanding reality, perhaps another will become available to me?" As stories and possibilities emerge, they can keep moving forward instead of running back to the old paradigm or literally back inside the church building.

Jesus constantly presented people with probing questions, invitations into curiosity, and images of an alternative, God-shaped community of love. We can help each other to cultivate that holy curiosity and imagine new ways of being, too. Tammerie Day says the point is to "discover alternatives"—the world is not what you always thought, but it could be something else, and you can see what that something might be.[15]

The truth here makes intuitive sense. Of course people won't simply surrender their privilege and power, and they certainly won't let go of the narratives, institutions, and structures that ground their lives, if there's no compelling alternative on offer. That's why so many men are working to fashion identities apart from "toxic masculinity." I am grateful to White scholars like Janet Helms[16] and the team responsible for Racial Equity Tools;[17] they're helping White folks to imagine honest, healthy, anti-racist ways of inhabiting White identity. Learn more about their work and find links to a resource for "Developing a Positive White Identity" in the Reflection & Action Guide that accompanies this book.

I know some people will argue that positive White identity is an oxymoron. They maintain White is the color of the oppressor, and there is no way to be White apart from participation in the domination system that is Whiteness. I hang on to the hope that, when people with privilege discover alternatives to life as they've known it—especially alternatives like the community of love Jesus inaugurated—they are better able to allow structures built for supremacy, domination, and empire to crack and to join in building something else.

Step 4: Engage in Critical Analysis

If step 1 was truly seeing reality, now it's time to interrogate it. Consider questions like these at the critical analysis stage in the journey:[18]

- Why are things the way they are?
- Why does this injustice exist?
- Who benefits from this injustice, structurally and personally?
- What are the systems, institutions, and structures humming in the background or overhead, beyond my sight but powerfully shaping reality?
- What would Jesus have to say about this situation?

I like describing this process as "interrogation" because sometimes we need to get confrontational about the way we investigate our world and hold ourselves accountable. Ask, "Why?" and keep asking it until you see what's really at stake, who built it, why they built it, who benefits, who suffers, and how it compares to the reign of God and contributes to God's beloved community.

The journey does not stop with asking questions about the world, institutions, and systems around you. Eventually, Day says, you and your community must turn to acknowledge your relationship to these systems, in what is known as *stance analysis*.[19] At this phase, you and your community might ask:

- What can I/we no longer stand?
- With whom will I/we stand? For what will I/we stand?
- Where can I/we no longer stand?
- What cost am I / are we willing to bear?

This deeper reckoning is the precursor to movement, especially for institutions that have so fully allied with the ways of empire and control. Given what we know, given where we have been and where we see God's Spirit leading, where will we stand?

The point is not to record detailed answers on a spreadsheet, check off a box, close the book, and return to normal life. It's not even just waking up and seeing things differently. By seriously interrogating reality and arriving at clear convictions, you are discerning where and how God is calling you to stand and move in the world. You are ultimately gauging your own willingness to lose your life for the sake of the gospel of love.

7

Gain Your Life—Solidarity

No man is an island, entire of itself; every man is a piece of the continent, a part of the main. If a clod be washed away by the sea, Europe is the less, as well as if a promontory were, as well as if a manor of thy friend's or of thine own were: any man's death diminishes me, because I am involved in mankind, and therefore never send to know for whom the bell tolls; it tolls for thee.
—John Donne, "Meditation 17"

Tears leaked from my eyes the day I recited those words in front of Rusha Sams's English class at Bearden High School in Knoxville, Tennessee. I wasn't yet baptized and didn't fully grasp the idea of God. I knew Donne was a seventeenth-century English poet; no one mentioned he was also an Anglican priest who served as dean of St. Paul's Cathedral in London (or if Mrs. Sams had told us, I didn't care at the time). I only knew Donne had finally put words to a truth I knew in my gut: *we are bound.* If I think the bell tolls to mark someone else's death or loss, if I imagine my privilege or distance shields me from their pain, I'm wrong. You can't gain your life while your neighbor loses hers. Whatever wounds one part of the body wounds the whole. Regardless of what the persuasive voice of self-centrism tells us, I knew the truth: *we are bound.*

I learned this early on. In the small Kentucky city where I grew up, it worked to be the skinny, nerdy, Black girl that Whites could point to and say, "She's not like the rest of 'them.'" My brother Gary's experience was unlike mine in every way. Though he was only five years older, he was a young Black man with a late diagnosis of dyslexia and attention deficit hyperactivity disorder. Even if he was popular with his peers, his teachers assumed the worst as soon as he walked into any classroom. Police officers would do the same as he got older.

I hadn't mastered terms like "oppression," "racism," or "elitism," but I could see forces arrayed against Gary that I did not have to face myself. I knew I had a choice: I could play it safe and watch out for myself, or I could let the injustice break my heart and learn how to oppose the systems attempting to shackle my brother and anybody else who was inconvenient, unwanted, or simply non-White (including me if I didn't play nice). The first time Gary called from the police station, scared and confused because he hadn't done anything wrong and it all just happened so fast and they had him on the ground and then in the back of the cruiser and then in a cell—I felt the injustice break my fourteen-year-old heart.

It broke again in college. My freshman year at Wake Forest University in North Carolina, there was one out gay student on a campus with about thirty-five hundred undergraduates. Somehow, over the course of four years, God saw fit to send not one, not two, but three of my best friends tumbling out of the closet.

I will never forget the evening Keith entered my dorm room and popped in a cassette tape of Diana Ross singing "I'm Coming Out."

It took a while for the penny to drop, but as my eyes got rounder and his smile went from tentative to broad, the tears came. I was hopeful. I was curious. Mostly, I was scared for him and wondered how he would love and even survive as a Black, gay, young man in the South. He told me, "I don't need you to be scared. If you love me, use your power and stand with me."

Keith's charge blurred together with John Donne's—"Never ask for whom the bell tolls; it tolls for thee." How could anybody follow through on a call like this? My religion classes provided a hint: that's where I first heard the word "solidarity."

From Kenosis to Solidarity

Solidarity is love crossing the borders drawn by self-centrism, in order to enter into the situation of the other, for the purpose of mutual relationship and struggle that heals us all and enacts God's beloved community.

Solidarity is the voice that finally comprehends: "You are not the same as me, but part of you lives in me. Your freedom and mine were always inextricably entwined. Now I see it, and because of what I see, I choose to live differently. I will go there, with you, for your sake and for my own."

I see solidarity in the witness of Vida Scudder, who found that the gospel didn't make sense outside of relationship with the poor. Why? Because, she noted, "The disinherited and the humble were the first to profess the faith, and the formulas of that faith are theirs. The prosperous are those who now profess it, and the formulas are strange upon their lips."[1]

I see it in Jonathan Daniels, who wrote to friends in the North that he felt, inexplicably, as if "my heart is black."[2] He lost his original life and uncovered his own full humanity in relationship with suffering Black folks in Alabama.

I have also seen moments of solidarity in the Episcopal Church's witness alongside LGBTQ siblings over the last fifty years, even in the face of lawsuits and global shaming. I've heard shades of it in the stories of the General Convention Special Program, the church's first venture toward reparations and mutual relationship with Black communities in the 1960s and 1970s. I've seen it at Standing Rock, where Episcopalians continue to walk with the Sioux Nation (many of whom are Episcopal) to resist government and corporate efforts to build a pipeline that would desecrate sacred lands. And I've seen it on the U.S.–Mexico border, where Episcopalians risk arrest to head out into the desert and offer a cup of water to people who are today the face of Jesus.

Kenosis, and its actions of losing your life, cracking open, embracing disruption, releasing control—these are each only one part of the equation. We let go of one life in order to take up new life, the life of the beloved. We release what we hoarded in order to receive gift upon gift from God. Our cracked-open hearts are at last roomy enough to hold the lives and hearts of others. We practice kenosis in preparation for solidarity.

Latin American liberation theologians are some of the best teachers about solidarity. In countries where the power of Roman Catholicism united with the forces of colonialism, empire, and domination, these wise sisters and brothers insisted that true Christianity demands loving relationship with and struggle alongside the poor, the persecuted, and those most like Jesus in their time. Peruvian theologian Gustavo Gutiérrez declared it boldly:

> A spirituality of liberation will center on a conversion to the neighbor, the oppressed person, the exploited social class, the despised ethnic group, the dominated country. . . . Our conversion to the Lord implies this conversion to the neighbor. To be converted is to commit oneself lucidly, realistically, and concretely to the process of the liberation of the poor and

oppressed. . . . To be converted is to know and experience the fact that, contrary to the laws of physics, we can stand straight, according to the gospel, only when our center of gravity is outside ourselves.[3]

We usually think of conversion as the first step in becoming a Christian. If you truly want to move into loving relationship with God, Gutiérrez argued, you will be converted again and again toward loving relationship with the oppressed who struggle for freedom and wholeness. Recentering outside ourselves and with the most dominated and despised people is actually the way to abundant life.

Conversion is not a head trip. It moves your heart and body into deeper, loving relationship with others, especially with neighbors on the underside of empire, where even more love and freedom await. As I discovered with my brother and again with my college friends, and as Paul illustrates in 1 Corinthians 12, love is the conductor that carries the pain of the other across so it becomes your pain. Love binds us together.

Relationship like this is central to the practice of solidarity. Latina theologian Ada María Isasi-Díaz sums up solidarity as "the union of kindreds who work together toward the unfolding of God's kin-dom."[4] The bottom line is not who wins or loses the struggle, or even who secures enough allies to flip the power dynamic. Isasi-Díaz wants us to see that the loving, sacrificial friendship at the heart of solidarity is itself the antidote to sin and oppression.

Domination, control, and self- or group-centric behavior alienate and separate us from God, from each other, and from ourselves as beloved children of God. By contrast, embracing union with oppressed and despised peoples, placing any privilege you hold at the disposal of the movement to dismantle oppression and alienation and to restore balance and wholeness to human community—*this* solidary love is how we most closely and faithfully follow Jesus and join him in beloved community.

Now you can see why solidarity and kenosis are so closely yoked, and why they are essential to life in the reign of God. Once your heart has cracked open—or the heart of your institution has cracked open—you are positioned to give your life, privilege, and power away *specifically* for love of peoples who have suffered under the knee of oppression. This is how we all draw near to our crucified and risen God.

Jesus and Solidary Love

As God-among-us, Jesus demonstrates the way to move from a self-centric, self-seeking existence to solidarity. We've seen the pivotal Philippians 2 hymn that describes his journey: Jesus shared in God's nature, but he didn't cling to equality with God or use it for his own advantage. Instead, he divested and humbled himself, and became not just a human being but a slave. Then he descended even further and embraced the most humiliating death possible: execution on a cross.

On the one hand, this is a picture of kenosis, because Jesus gave up privilege to draw near to us. But his passion is sparked by the pain and hope he sees in our midst. Indeed, what we know of Jesus is that he was particularly insistent about relationship with the most vulnerable people: children, the poor, widows, strangers, prostitutes. He dwelled among those who suffer because they were least loved and thus most in need of God's public, passionate love to restore them to the place of equal belovedness that is our human birthright. They were the most willing to stretch their hands out to God and receive the gifts God longed to give to all of creation.

I use the word "passionate" here intentionally. There's no more accurate way to describe Jesus's love for humanity and especially for human beings on the margins. It was passion that drove him to look up at Zaccheus the tax collector, literally perched in a tree (talk about the margins), and to say, "Come down! I want to visit your house" (Luke 19:1–10). It was passion that stirred Jesus to linger with the Samaritan woman at the well, where they shared stories and questions in the full heat of the day and in the sight of the authorities who couldn't wait to accuse Jesus of impurity (John 4:4–30). Passion made him embrace the presence of children others wanted to send away (Matthew 19:13–15).

Jesus didn't just come to be with humanity or just to love all of humanity in general. He came to share God's love specifically with people who had been robbed of it, and he proved that love by being one of those despised people himself. Kelly Brown Douglas challenges us to recognize where Jesus would stand today. "The crucified class in the first-century Roman world was the same as the lynched class today. It consisted of those who were castigated and demonized as well as those who defied the status quo."[5] That non-empire-identified space is the best place for Jesus to confront traditional, dominant conceptions of power and show us what God's love and freedom are all about.

Jesus didn't identify with the underside in a few cases. He chose the decentered and the rejected groups on the underside of empire again and again. As Christopher Duraisingh points out, "A central aspect of the story of Jesus is that he refuses to play the role of the dominant hero, but always moves to the margin and to places of solidarity with the oppressed."[6] The powers of empire and domination want to adopt Jesus for their own purposes, but anybody looking at him will see that's not where he chose to be. He didn't dislike the wealthy or powerful—note his compassion for the rich young man in Matthew 19. He loved him and everyone else with privilege enough to reveal for them the path to salvation: through identification with people who are poor, suffering, and despised at any given time in any given community.

Stewardship of Privilege

Solidarity is a matter of love. It is also clear-eyed and strategic. Jesus chose to identify with the most vulnerable peoples in love, but let's be honest—his choice wouldn't have mattered so much if he were not God-among-us. As I think about privileged people of all sorts who could have ducked behind the shield of privilege but instead put their lives on the line, I'm reminded of this unavoidable truth: regardless of how you or I feel or think about privilege, the dominant culture has already decided some lives have greater value. When those lives are at risk, the powers take note.

In study after study, scientists have noted that White subjects consistently rate White pain as more severe than Black pain.[7] In addition, when White people observe a Black person going through the same physical experience as a White person, the White observers don't exhibit the same involuntary stress response—Black pain literally doesn't affect these White subjects as strongly.[8] Maybe they think we are physically stronger and can bear more pain. Maybe some primordial switch doesn't trip to indicate, "Hey, that's one of my people." Whatever the cause, we have scientific proof that in a White-dominated society, more hearts break when a White person suffers.

This is the nature of self-centric systems that privilege one group over the rest—the dominant group's life has greater value, its choices are presumed legitimate, and its suffering garners compassion. (For the record, that's why we have to specifically say "Black Lives Matter"; in a White-dominant system, Black lives do *not* matter as much as others.)

Solidarity takes this fact into account, and then transforms privilege into a tool to dismantle the master's house. Picture something like spiritual jujitsu: you can take hold of the power of privilege and turn it back on itself, to disarm the very thing it was designed to protect. I call this *stewardship of privilege*, and I am convinced it is one of the keys to practicing kenosis and solidarity in real life.[9]

Why is stewardship of privilege so important? First of all, as a straight person who seeks to be in solidarity with LGBTQIIA+ friends I dearly love, I cannot simply wake one day and declare, "I don't want straight privilege. I'm giving it back." The system grants it to me without my asking, just as it values White lives more than the lives of people of color. If these are the facts on the ground, what am I going to do about it? What am I going to do with it?

The other problem with simply dismissing privilege is that most of what we call privileges are basic human rights. It's a privilege to not be viewed as a threat by your own government and its agents, but should it be? Shouldn't we all enjoy the privilege of loving as we've been led by our Creator, speaking in a meeting and being presumed competent, hearing music from our culture in church and not having others scoff, and having our differently cultured church gatherings be recognized as bona fide expressions of Christian life? I'm not looking forward to that great morning when no one has these privileges. In God's community of love, we all experience the conditions to thrive, and we sacrifice in order to create those conditions for one another. If you've got privilege, as Jesus did, don't use it for your own happiness or to elevate your circle; leverage it as part of Jesus's movement to ensure everyone flourishes.

That's where stewardship of privilege comes in. First, you take the non-clinging, open-hearted approach we discussed in the previous chapter on kenosis. Recognize the privilege but don't grab onto it or let it define you and control your reality. Get curious about it. Sit with those with whom you seek to be in solidarity, and together wonder: what if I laid my privilege and power at the feet of this community I love, for the sake of our shared liberation and beloved community? The grid that follows—titled "Stewardship of Privilege: Using Your Power as Jesus Used His"—is designed to illustrate some of the possibilities for action and how Jesus leads the way.

Stewardship of Privilege:
Using Your Power as Jesus Used His

Jesus loved extravagantly: his friends, his enemies, and God.	**LOVE** the face and voice of God you see and hear in the presence of others.
In Jesus, God came among human beings, lived, wept, and died with us.	**CARE** and carry each other's burdens, even though your privilege means you could just turn the other way.
Jesus embraced human life, in its most humble and painful form.	**EMBRACE** uncomfortable spaces and experiences, and model vulnerability for others who share your privilege.
Jesus released control of his path so God could lead instead.	**SURRENDER** over-controlling behaviors and discern God's will in relationship with people who are oppressed.
Jesus risked it all by coming to be among us, loving when he was not loved, being open to correction, and refusing to curse those who hurt him.	**RISK** making the first move, sharing your own story, being wrong, appearing less than perfect, and receiving the anger of people who've been hurt by systems that protect you.
On the highways and byways of Galilee and beyond, Jesus walked with people and offered his listening ear and heart.	**LISTEN** with love to the stories of people who are oppressed, exploited, and have been denied privileges and resources you have.
Jesus trusted a woman—Mary—to carry the message that he had risen from the dead.	**TRUST** the perspective and wisdom of people who are the least respected.

God, in uniting divinity with humanity through Jesus, actually raised humanity and deified us (Richard Hooker).	**CELEBRATE** the cultures, gifts, and lives of groups who have been silenced or devalued.
Jesus promised to intercede on our behalf and carry our prayers to his Father.	**SPEAK** hard truths that people who share your privilege can hear from you.
Jesus incurred the wrath of the domination system because he stood with the oppressed.	**SUFFER** the displeasure and even the anger of the systems that privilege you, by stepping outside their bounds.
Jesus lived simply and encouraged people to look into their bags, share their possessions, and feed one another . . . and there was plenty.	**SACRIFICE** possessions and resources for the sake of love, so that no one has too much and no one goes without.
Jesus welcomes us into the relationship he shares with his Father and the Holy Spirit.	**SHARE** privileged access and usher less privileged people into spaces and relationships that advance liberation for the whole.
Jesus turned everything upside down, disobeyed unjust rules, and honored "the least of these," in order to bring all things back into right relationship.	**DISMANTLE** systems that reinforce domination, distribute privilege unequally, and diminish human life.

Note: Sometimes you're the one with power and sometimes you're the one on the underside. Your community may also collectively hold certain privileges you don't personally possess. So approach this practice creatively, understanding that most all of us have some form of privilege we can turn over as blessing for others and for the whole.

Working with this grid, I've found people who have been unaware can begin to imagine different ways of living. Fearmongering voices may say, "People on the bottom want to take everything from you and leave you with nothing in order to punish you for being successful." In this grid, you see how faith leads us away from those punishing, self-centric, zero-sum models and toward trust, generosity, celebration, wholeness, sacrifice, and justice. For many of us, this is what solidarity looks like when we live it out practically.

Yes, there is risk involved. Yes, you and your church will lose some of what you had identified as your life. No, it will not destroy you entirely, thanks to the grace of God and the power of the Spirit working in you. And yes, we are following Jesus.

8

Walk in Love—Discipleship

Discipleship is an invitation to follow
Jesus into a new community.
—David Swanson[1]

We've wrestled with plenty of big ideas and knotty issues on this journey. But perhaps none is more important than this: discipleship. If a defining challenge for majority American churches is that we have overwhelmingly aligned with cultures of domination and social control and advanced our own interests and kingdoms over the reign of God—and yes, that is the central issue I've tried to tackle here—then the solution isn't chiefly a matter of anti-racism training, online liturgies, and drive-up soup kitchens. It comes down to asking ourselves what will we place at the center of our lives and who will we follow? That's a question only discipleship can answer.

A *disciple* is simply one who follows, learns, and patterns their life after another. Everybody is a disciple of something or someone. I would invite you now to take a moment and wonder: of what or of whom are you a disciple? Who or what shapes your life and teaches you? Most Christians quickly reply, "Jesus!" But does he? I fear that dominant American Christian churches are by and large designed to shape cooperative, peaceful, and kind residents and consumers, and only occasionally form vibrant, self-giving, world-changing followers of Jesus of Nazareth who love God and love our neighbors, strangers, and even our enemies as we love ourselves.

How did we land here? Most historians point to the pivotal moment in 312 CE when the emperor Constantine converted to Christianity *and* Christianity converted to become an ally and instrument of the emperor. From then on, with too few exceptions, the way of empire, domination, established order, and cultural supremacy has eclipsed much of what Jesus inaugurated some two thousand years ago.

Movements have risen to set Christians back on the way of Jesus. Monastics, mystics, and reformers have lit the fires when they dimmed. We've invoked some of those leaders in these very pages. But the siren song of empire is seductive, and oppressive powers can morph and slide just out of view so smoothly we don't realize they're still running the show. They've been especially adept at weaving the established order and White superiority into the core of dominant American Christianity, to the point where it's tough to know where one ends and the other begins. It takes disruption to break the hold of these powers and propel us back into Jesus's arms. It takes being cracked open.

Many of us are praying that the church has indeed arrived at a point when—thanks to disruption and decline—Christians have less to lose or to prove and can choose to pour ourselves out in love for the world. Now that we've been cracked open and we see more of what's at the church's core, we can reimagine with God a Christianity that is not built on self-centrism, domination, and White supremacy. Imagine recentering on the God we know in Jesus. Imagine becoming practicing communities that follow Jesus and embody his community of love.

The forces of empire and establishment will tell you that's a worthy cause but impossible in this day and age. They are wrong. What it takes is disciples who together follow Jesus in his Way of Love, lean fully into the Spirit that animated him, and try to do what he did and live as he lived, so that we, our communities, and the whole world might become more like him.

A Way for Us All

Early in his tenure as presiding bishop of the Episcopal Church, Michael Curry brought together a group of advisers and asked us to help him to lead the church more deeply into the heart of Jesus. We spoke avidly of small groups and practicing communities, and we were just as fervent about subverting empire and dismantling systems of oppression. We sensed something could break open in the next twenty to forty years, and we needed to be ready. The group drafted a rule of life known as the Way of Love: seven practices for Jesus-centered life. Starting in mid-2018, church groups of every size and location began to take up the Way of Love and make it their own. That movement continues to this day.

It has been life-giving to watch Episcopalians take Jesus at his word, trusting that we disciples could form communities like his if we open to the Spirit and follow on his simple way:

1. TURN again and again to God.
2. LEARN Jesus's ways through scripture and holy reading.
3. PRAY and dwell intentionally with God every day.
4. WORSHIP God weekly through community praise, thanksgiving, and petition.
5. BLESS one another by giving our lives away in love.
6. GO across borders to join in solidarity and heal brokenness.
7. REST in God's grace, because the revolution is not ultimately up to us.

The Episcopal Church's adoption of the Way of Love tapped into a wider effort across the Anglican Communion to reanimate and reground ourselves in God through intentional discipleship. The Anglican Consultative Council—the global church's chief decision-making body—declared a ten-year "Season of Intentional Discipleship" and encouraged churches everywhere to take up Jesus-Shaped Life, a pathway for imitating and being formed by Jesus's way of life.[2]

I was honored to sit at the tables responsible for crafting and introducing both the Way of Love and Jesus-Shaped Life, so I know both pathways flow from a common yearning. From Lusaka to Manila, Kuala Lumpur to Kansas, we hoped to see Christians centering our lives on God and praying to have our lives shaped like Jesus's, rather than following the prevailing cultures of commerce, racial supremacy, colonialism, and self-centrism. We longed for what I've heard Presiding Bishop Curry describe: a reverse Copernican revolution, one that would place God at the center, rather than keep the world revolving around our individual selves and groups. We were crazy enough to imagine God might someday counter what Constantine had done all those centuries ago and take back God's church.

We thought we'd get an opening in a couple of decades. God apparently had something else in mind.

Just a couple of months before I began work on this book, as the scale of the pandemic and racial reckonings became apparent, I sat once again with advisers for both the Way of Love and Jesus-Shaped Life. We were full of anxiety and hope; I could practically hear the *Hamilton* soundtrack in the background of our Zoom calls, charging up the revolutionaries. If our churches were ever going to follow Jesus in his way of self-giving love, if we had a chance of decentering off self and empire and recentering on God, if we hoped to turn and become even a little more the beloved community Jesus inaugurated—this might be our shot.

Today I'm more convinced than ever that God is up to something, and that this time the way of Jesus could be more compelling than the empty promises of empire, self-centrism, and domination. What have we got to lose? And what more could we gain?

In these final pages, we will explore together the seven practices of the Way of Love, weaving in wisdom you've seen throughout the book so far. At www.episcopalchurch.org/wayoflove, you can discover a rich array of resources to support your practice. Here I am eager to share reflections and concrete steps designed to help individuals, congregations, and entire church bodies to follow Jesus, lose the life bound up with empire and domination, and be reborn as disciples who seek God's community of love.

TURN Again and Again to God

The first words Jesus preached in Mark 1 were a call to turn: "The time is fulfilled, and the kingdom of God has come near; repent and believe in the good news" (Mark 1:15). The key word is "repent," or *metanoia* in Greek, and it means a turning of the heart or mind away from one path and toward another. Disruption and decline have cracked us open, and we have the opportunity to gain freedom from self-centrism as individuals, races, institutions, and nations, and to turn and rediscover God as the true center of our lives.

As individuals, we can choose to turn after something wakes us to reality or simply breaks our hearts. Once you begin to learn and feel more fully, and experience your reality and consciousness shifting, you can start to ask yourself questions like: What are the true loves and concerns around which I've organized my life? What do I actually come to church for? Have I placed God in a convenient space, to be consulted when I need some help but otherwise not getting too much in the way? How have I and my church benefited from empire, oppression, or cultural/racial supremacy, or simply turned away from these realities? Queries like these can stir a reckoning.

The good news is that God gives us innumerable chances to turn. That's the power of grace. So even if I choose to keep my head down and keep pretending a little longer, God won't close the door on me. Every moment, God is waiting for me to make the next choice for more than myself, my group, or my limited circle of concern.

Congregations and institutions can be a great practice ground for turning. Imagine gatherings where people regularly offer testimony about how we're facing reality and how we're learning to slowly turn toward God. Do it as part of the sermon or in small group breakouts during online coffee hour. Learn from Alcoholics Anonymous and twelve-step programs that know this model intimately. Regular practices of storytelling and accountability help us to build a culture capable of graceful turning, where people can bring their imperfect, struggling, hopeful, vulnerable selves into community.

Publicly sharing about how we're turning also prepares communities for collective turning and repentance. Lots of churches refer to the (other) seven last words: "But we've never done it that way." We laugh, but aversion to conversion isn't healthy. If your congregation or institution is terrified of change or being wrong, how can you begin to turn from the lure of empire and establishment? Many congregations have taken on the humbling work of investigating their history and complicity in colonialism, slavery, and ongoing systems of domination. They intentionally engage in confession, repentance, seeking forgiveness, and reparation of what they've broken or what's been broken on their behalf. All these steps require flexibility, curiosity, and grace to keep turning toward God.

What a blessing that so many church folks have learned to turn in this time of upheaval. People who never dreamt they'd speak the words "Black Lives Matter" have joined the chorus on the streets. Bishops who defended the gates around the communion table have released local leaders to discover new ways to gather and nourish God's people. We've surprised ourselves by our capacity to turn. Now it needs to become part of our daily life as followers of Jesus, not merely an exception for extraordinary times.

LEARN Jesus's Ways through Scripture and Holy Reading

The only way to be a disciple is by learning the way of the one you follow and trying on their life for yourself. Through scripture and holy reading, we learn the life, teachings, and ways of Jesus and of the disciples who've followed him before us.

Be warned: the more you learn about Jesus, the more you'll realize what a risk taker he was. He constantly embraced failure, broke unjust rules, forgave those who trespassed against him, built alternative communities of love, and prioritized the witness and needs of the least empowered. Eventually, he took up the cross and lost his life in order to gain even greater life. It's strange, radical, and wonderful, and it's all straight from the mouth and life of Jesus.

If anyone tries to tell you God endorses domination and oppression—and church history and present times are rife with just that message—look instead to Jesus. He shows us just how much God longs to upend power structures, so that no one dominates or crucifies anybody else ever again. Following Jesus, we see God's desire to loosen our grip on our possessions and identities, so that we hold onto God alone.

Our model for kenosis is Jesus, the one who gave away his life for love: at the incarnation, through his life and ministry, and all the way to the cross. We know solidarity because we see Jesus entering into the fullness of humanity, particularly hurting and despised humanity, so he could love and suffer and rise again right by our side.

We love the God who is known to us in the Father, Son, and Holy Spirit. And we are called Christians because we follow Jesus Christ into the heart of that trinitarian God. As we learn his ways through scripture, we gain the necessary tools to discern God's Spirit moving in the whole of scripture and across traditions, cultures, and generations. As we come to know him, and in knowing grow to love him and to understand the depth of his love for us, we will be better able to imitate his gracious, generous, risk-taking, humble, loving, and radical ways and join him in building the community of love that God intends.

PRAY and Dwell Intentionally with God Every Day

In his letter to the community in Thessalonica, Paul urges disciples to pray without ceasing. It could sound like a heavy burden, but there are so many ways we pray. We pray as we read scripture. We pray in the midst of worship, and as we minister and serve outside of church. We pray with our feet as we struggle for justice. We pray for grace and forgiveness to turn away from obsession with self, possessions, and control. We offer our lives to God as one unending prayer.

At base, prayer is any way that we listen, share, and dwell intentionally with God. As we look to the witness of people who have embraced kenosis and solidarity and challenged the empire's hold on Christianity, we will see people who prayed their way through and invite us to do the same. You may recall Vida Scudder, the Victorian socialist who taught at an elite women's college and lived among Boston's most poor and desperate. Her public ministry was remarkable, but she would tell you it was an outgrowth of intercessory prayer, the kind of prayer that places God and neighbor first.[3] The community she shared with her friends—the Society of Companions of the Holy Cross—is still alive today, with vowed companions who live around the world, each one dedicated to reconciliation and transformation. Both practices are grounded in a first commitment to prayer.

Whether we are engaged in intercessory prayer or other forms, prayer takes us out of ourselves and places us and all that we offer in God's hands. Empire, colonialism, and self-centrism have effectively replaced our reliance on God with institutions and designated representatives of God. In prayer—individually and also in groups, from a book, as well as when it's spontaneous or silent—we practice listening closely and discerning directly with the God we know as Creator, Christ, and Holy Spirit. Prayer takes me and my particular group out of the driver's seat and reinstalls God at the center. Reoriented in this way, I may actually be able to recognize and follow Jesus in his Way of Love.

WORSHIP God Weekly in Community

COVID-19 has upended life as we know it, and there are no guarantees that by the time this book is in your hands church folk will have access to their buildings and be gathered for anything resembling worship. I will take a risk and say this may be a gift from God.

Don't get me wrong. I am in awe of the herculean effort clergy and church leaders have invested in worship during a pandemic, and I grieve for the extra labor, the uncertainty, and the sheer exhaustion so many have weathered. Still, I would be lying if I said worship prior to COVID-19 was an ideal form to which we should return as quickly as possible. As beautiful as they can be, liturgical traditions—including my own Episcopal Church's traditions—serve as some of the strongest yokes to White supremacy, domination, and established order. If dominant American Christianity is controlled by the "Euro-tribal churches" described in chapter 1, then worship is where that tribalism plays out most fully.

For lots of Episcopalians, and I imagine for many of our peers, worship is the draw that gets and keeps you in the fold. Some people would rather criticize Jesus than the liturgy. Maybe that's the seat of the problem, and why following Jesus may demand a reorientation to our worship.

Worship—like prayer—should place us in right relationship with God and each other. It should seek to enact the grace and breadth of the beloved community, teach us to live and love like Jesus, make us feel at once humbled and elevated into the arms of God, and send us out as God's ambassadors to help envelop the world with the love and blessing we've received.

In too many instances, majority American Christian worship reflects the dominant group's cultural, racial, and class identities, and empowers a small group of people to speak with and about God on behalf of the whole. Recent racial reckonings have forced some tough but welcome conversations about why dominant American Christian worship is so identified with Whiteness and empire. People of color and people from less privileged class backgrounds have for decades been honest about our sadness and alienation inside our own churches. The predominant images of God, hymns, musical instruments, architecture, and the overall tone and style of worship in these congregations clearly communicate the superiority and centrality of Whiteness and the rightness of domination. I say this not as a judgment or even as a complaint, but as a statement of observable fact.

In the Episcopal Church, our history as chaplain to the ruling classes adds an extra layer of uniformity, perfectionism, and quintessentially English sobriety to much of our worship. You would expect the church of empire and establishment to strictly enforce worship regulations and culturally determined standards of excellence, and indeed we do.

If our worship were more in sync with practicing Jesus's Way of Love on the path toward becoming beloved community, it might resemble the church in the midst of pandemic: decentered from buildings and familiarity, and recentered in imaginative, often marginal spaces where God's Spirit might break through and where newcomers are on closer to equal footing with old-timers (since we're all figuring it out together).

First, we would apply the spiritual principle of non-attachment and non-clinging to our buildings. These beautiful, alabaster jars within which we store the things of God have broken open; we do not have to piece them back together the way they were. Some people might worship in glorious cathedrals and stately sanctuaries, but others would gather in homes, community centers, and online spaces, and each would have equal value as a practicing Christian community. Bishops and liturgical leaders would allow far greater latitude to local communities seeking to worship God and share the gospel of Jesus Christ in the cultural language appropriate to their contexts.

We could release some of our dependency on credentialing and certifying every aspect of ministry. Imagine more home altars, more lay preaching, and intentional small group formation led by laypeople for laypeople. When it comes to music, the organ would no longer be the gold standard against which church musicianship is measured. Instead, acapella singing and simpler accompaniment would complement (and not overwhelm) the sound of human voices raised to make music and make community. Moves like this would also open up the range of cultural expressions that sound like "church."

I take heart in the wisdom of Juan Oliver, who gives us all the permission we need to remove worship from the museum shelves and free it from oppressive, controlling forces:

> [L]iturgical do's and don'ts are relative, for they are determined by culture, not by God, and so they are—as the Reformers knew so well, fallible and like the Church herself, always in need of being reformed. Even the structure of the Eucharistic Prayer itself is not written up in heaven. But our names are, each in its own language.[4]

BLESS One Another by Giving Our Lives Away in Love

How will the world recognize a group of Christians? Jesus said: "By this everyone will know that you are my disciples, if you have love for one another" (John 13:35). He hoped we would extravagantly, unselfishly bless each other. No group will perfectly fulfill Jesus's hope, but he has given us his Spirit so we have the power to move in that direction.

If you wonder how we can practically become people and communities of blessing—that is, people who give our lives away for the sake of love—reflect again on the Stewardship of Privilege chart on pages 114 and 115. It describes a concrete way for us to release our

grip on what we possess, and to place it in the service of God's dream
and God's people. Below is an abbreviated version:

- LOVE the face and voice of God in others.
- CELEBRATE the cultures, gifts, and lives of rejected groups.
- CARE and carry each other's burdens.
- EMBRACE uncomfortable spaces and experiences.
- SURRENDER overcontrolling behaviors.
- RISK making the first move, sharing your own stories, and
  being wrong.
- LISTEN with love to the stories of people who do not share
  your privilege.
- SACRIFICE possessions and resources for the sake of love.
- SHARE access to privileged spaces and relationships.

People and communities of blessing choose generosity over domination, celebration over humiliation, mutuality over chauvinism. We
resist the way of empire, because it regards one culture and its practices, aesthetics, rules, and institutions as the best of all and ideal for
everyone, and because it places human creation above the revealed
will and way of God. We resist the urge to build up and hoard power,
possession, and privilege, because—as Jesus showed us—real love
gives itself away as bold, generous blessing to others.

GO Across Borders to Join in Solidarity and Heal Brokenness

The practice of "go" shares a lot in common with the practice of
"bless." The main difference is that going takes the blessing beyond
your circle, across borders and divisions, and into the world for the
explicit purpose of repairing what's broken, bearing God's justice, and
forming wider and wider circles of beloved community.

The story of the apostle Philip and the Ethiopian eunuch (Acts
8:26–40) illustrates how we might go in the way of Jesus. In the
online Reflection & Action Guide that accompanies this book, you'll

find a fuller telling of the story and concrete practices that match up with Philip and the eunuch's journey. For now, let's briefly learn from these two disciples about how to "go."

- As the passage opens, an angel tells the apostle Philip to go to the wilderness road from Jerusalem to Gaza. Philip is willing to *follow the Spirit's lead.*

- The Spirit sends him to *draw near difference.* Philip sees an Ethiopian eunuch riding in a chariot. Remember that "Ethiopian" signified a dark-skinned African. In addition, as a eunuch, he couldn't enter the temple (Deuteronomy 23). An Ethiopian eunuch occupied the margins of gender, sexual, ethnic, and religious identity.

- The Spirit says, "*Show up.* Go where he is. Offer your presence." Philip doesn't hesitate or worry about rejection.

- When he arrives, he listens and notices the eunuch reading from the prophet Isaiah. So Philip asks him, "Do you understand this?" Philip is willing to *lead with curiosity* rather than his own knowledge or agenda.

- By listening, he has the chance to *notice pain, yearning, and wisdom* in the eunuch, who shares this telling passage from Isaiah: "In his humiliation justice was denied him." The eunuch then asks, "About whom was the prophet speaking?"

- Philip goes on to *connect the stories.* He likely weaves Jesus's story together with the eunuch's own suffering and longing. What good news, to know God has felt the same pain, that God is with him and wills him to be free, whole, and beloved.

- Once the eunuch hears the good news, he exclaims, "Look, here's water! What's stopping you from baptizing me?" The ritual authorities would have raised a hundred objections, but Philip listens to a higher authority: God. Philip is willing to *transgress for the sake of love.* The two exit the chariot and enter the waters. On this day, both would *be converted* to the life and way of Jesus.

- Afterward, they *go rejoicing where the Spirit leads next.* The eunuch is now an ambassador of Christ's reconciliation and healing, and Philip is sent to new towns, more ready than ever to share the good news.

Followers of Jesus don't stand still, and we don't stay at the center waiting for centripetal force to draw all the people and resources inside to us. We go out beyond comfort, knowing, and certainty. We go when and where the Holy Spirit sends us.

REST in God's Grace, Because the Revolution Is Not Ultimately Up to Us

The logic of empire says we have to control everything we survey, and then it sets creation spinning around us as the axis, which then forces us to churn and dash to stay on top of it all. But we're not the ones controlling creation, nor are we at its center. The church doesn't control all the levers or hold all the answers, either. The world, including the church, belongs to God.

If the world belongs to God, our first responsibility is not to dominate, but to find out where God is already active and move in that direction. I picture Jesus walking on the water, drawing Peter out to meet him and saying, "Don't be afraid. Don't look down in fear and panic. Keep your head up. The waters are rushing, but you will not sink." I see Jesus gazing with compassion at anxious disciples and telling them, "Take my yoke upon you and learn from me; for I am gentle and humble in heart, and you will find rest for your souls" (Matthew 11:29–30).

Jesus calls us toward restoration and rest. We are yoked to God and one another, if we would only look around. We can halt our incessant struggling and controlling, and the nightmare of self-centrism and my-group-against-the-rest can end. Breathe.

Freed and centered in this way, we find that even when we work hard, we are not hard-bitten. Even when we engage in deep struggle, we are not struggling. There is a measure of rest and grace when we trust that God's power working in us really will do infinitely more than we could ask or imagine (Ephesians 3:20).

What does a church that is not centered on empire, domination, White supremacy, and social control look like? Look to Jesus. He made plain the way to follow him and the kind of countercultural communities of love we could be if we did. He gave us practices—Turn, Learn, Pray, Worship, Bless, Go, Rest—that would form us internally into his likeness *and* enable us to embody him in the world. Then he granted us access to the same Spirit that powered him.

No matter how many times we've turned the other way, Jesus stands before us full of grace and hope, offering opportunities to follow him and become a different kind of people and a different kind of community. He opens up the way to be reborn as disciples who are centered on God and becoming beloved community. This could be our moment to finally say "yes."

CONCLUSION

God Bless the Cracks

*Allow me to say, in conclusion, notwithstanding the
dark picture I have this day presented of the state of the
nation, I do not despair of this country. . . . [M]y spirit
is also cheered by the obvious tendencies of the age.*
—Frederick Douglass[1]

No one asks to be cracked open or disrupted. No church seeks to decline in membership or stature. Most people don't go looking for experiences that will humble them and break their hold on a treasured identity and culture. We did not choose to land here in this wilderness; we were shoved by pandemic, racial reckoning, decline, and economic and social disruption. But now that we're here, humbled and open, we have a choice and a chance.

If you're sick of the way empire and the dominant American church culture weave around each other like a snake eating its tail . . .

If you're tired of Sunday morning being the most segregated hour of the week . . .

If you dread the inevitable next video of a cop killing an unarmed Black or Brown person . . .

If you don't want to rebuild or shore up a church with White supremacy at its core . . .

If you're not leaving and you refuse to surrender to bitterness and despair . . .

If you know God has more love, more freedom, and more life in store for us, and you want to be part of making that dream real . . .

What will you do?

If you've come to this conclusion, I hope you're beginning to craft that picture of what's next for yourself, for your congregation or ministry, and for the wider communities of which we are a part. The Reflection & Action Guide at www.churchcrackedopen.com and churchpublishing.org/churchcrackedopen is designed to offer even more wisdom and support for your ongoing journey. But whatever God leads you toward, let it be more than church as it has been. Maya Angelou once advised: "Do the best you can until you know better. Then when you know better, do better." We know where we've been, and we know where God bids us go. By the power of God's Holy Spirit, I believe redemption is possible. I believe we can do and be better.

I shared that hope with Mark Bozzuti-Jones, a brilliant priest, poet, and friend, and he almost immediately responded with a new poem titled "The Cross and the Crown." These lines captured my heart, and I share them here with his permission:

> Let our jars be cracked open
> Let our lives be poured out
> Let our lives witness to those virtues, and vows, and gospel truth
> knowing that all we do and think and say and pray matter
> Crack a little further
>   every single day
> and let in the light
> the right
> the repentance

join hearts
>   in the wisdom and love
> and life
> prepared for cracked hearts
> from all eternity.

I pray that we can embrace each other's cracked hearts and the cracked-open pieces of God's church and take advantage of this rare opportunity to be reshaped into communities that actively, intentionally embody and witness to the reality of God's beloved community. As painful as it feels, God may even now be taking hold of the dismantled pieces and refashioning a community after God's own heart.

Does that statement sound like thinly veiled judgment or iconoclasm? It isn't meant to. I love God, the one who created, redeems, and sustains us through everything this world can send our way. I love the Christian faith and traditions we have received, and how they hold mystery, truth, and love and lead billions toward the heart of God. I have special love for the Episcopal Church, the peculiar, beautiful, broken, empire-identified branch of the Jesus Movement within which I have most fully experienced God's call and blessing.

I love the church the same way Frederick Douglass loved America: not in spite of its brokenness, not hiding from its truths, but taking what is and what could be and embracing it with deep love and fierce, unshaken hope. That's the kind of love our church cracked open needs right now. A love that gets frustrated and angry but keeps on going. A love that gets sad and tired but keeps on hoping. A love that's willing to smash our own jars and let the oil pour, because we trust God is creating something even more beautiful with those broken pieces.

How and when you choose to say "yes" to that invitation, know that you do not walk alone. We are companions, you and I. So walk in power, and travel with this blessing:

May the Spirit of God draw you out onto the wilderness road.
May she send you chasing chariots and smashing alabaster,
beyond all propriety.
May she bring you to dark-skinned eunuchs and Samaritan women
and young ones who dream wild dreams
and rich rulers who long to fit through the eye of the needle.
And may they receive you into their homes and their worlds,
so you might teach and convert one another.
And may you enter the waters of baptism together,
and die and rise in Christ together,
in the name of the Creator and of the Son and of the Holy Spirit.
Amen.

ACKNOWLEDGMENTS

When the Spirit tells you to write a book in seven weeks flat in the midst of a pandemic, and it happens, you're going to have a lot of people to thank on the other end. Even if my words in this section are brief, please know that I could have filled another ten pages with love, gratitude, and high-five Bitmojis:

To God, because you always make a way out of no way.

To Nancy Bryan, Ryan Masteller, and the Church Publishing team, for not blinking when I texted in late June to say, "I think I need to write a book. For the next cycle. I can have it to you by end of summer."

To the staff and leadership of the Domestic Foreign and Missionary Society of the Episcopal Church, for offering the prayers, patience, wisdom, back-up, sanity checks, and permission (Suzanne Baillie!) necessary for me to pursue this project; and especially to our fearless and faithful leader, Presiding Bishop Michael Curry, who said, "We need this. Go do it."

To Jane and John Gould, who shared their beautiful, empty lake house in Western Massachusetts and gave me seven weeks of peace to do the impossible.

To many friends and colleagues (lists like this are so dangerous!): Kelly Brown Douglas and Winnie Varghese (you made me do this); Gerry Cahill, Lynn Campbell, Eva Cavaleri, Courtney Cowart, Alessandra Cozzi, Julie Cudahy-Longmuir, Julie Hoplamazian, Gia Moreno, Tamara Plummer, and Calvin Sanborn (those texts kept me going); the Chiefs and Canons (y'all really are my church); Sarah Alphin, Tom Brackett, Jerusalem Greer, Anthony Guillen, Melanie

Mullen, Jeremy Tackett, and all of Team ERCC (you are my teachers); and Mark Bozzuti-Jones (your poetry brought out mine).

To Carrie Boren Headington and Dwight Zscheile, who took each chapter and gave me the kind of feedback writers dream of but almost never get.

To Bart Geissinger and Camp Washington in Morris, Connecticut, and David Fischer, for opening your doors when I needed sanctuary and inspiration at the end.

To my Facebook family, the thousands who prayed and pinged and reflected with me every step of the way—who says digital community isn't real community?

To my actual family, especially Mama Phyllis Spellers, who surrounded me with books and let her weird child be weird.

To Albert DeGrasse, beloved leader of Quaranteam 802 and a patient, smart, kind, not-woke-but-waking White guy who nodded as I read aloud (and loudly) from racist eighteenth-century vestry minutes, fed me fruit and veggies, did laundry, and built fires like a boss. Yeah, you, the one out there teaching the Doctrine of Discovery to seventh graders. The one who put that "Beloved Community" sign up over your classroom door. The one who agreed to marry me in the midst of this madness. You inspire me every day. Now let's get after it.

NOTES

Introduction: On Being Cracked Open

1. Andy Crouch, Kurt Keilhacker, and Dave Blanchard, "Leading Beyond the Blizzard: Why Every Organization Is Now a Startup," https://journal.praxislabs.org/leading-beyond-the-blizzard-why-every-organization-is-now-a-startup-b7f32fb278ff, accessed August 13, 2020.

Chapter 1: The Reality of Disruption and Decline

1. Martin Luther King Jr., "1966 Ware Lecture: Don't Sleep Through the Revolution," Unitarian Universalist Association General Assembly, May 18, 1966, https://www.uua.org/ga/past/1966/ware, accessed November 15, 2020.
2. Episcopal membership peaked at 3.4 million people in 1966 and has fallen steeply since then. Official counts in 2019 report about 1.8 million members. See https://www.generalconvention.org/parochial reportresults and Association of Religion Data Archives, https://www.thearda.com/Denoms/D_849.asp, both accessed November 13, 2020.
3. "Status of Global Christianity, 2020, in the Context of 1900–2050," Center for the Study of Global Christianity, Gordon-Conwell Theological Seminary, https://www.gordonconwell.edu/center-for-global-christianity/wp-content/uploads/sites/13/2020/02/Status-of-Global-Christianity-2020.pdf, accessed October 11, 2020.

4. David Kinnaman and Gabe Lyons, *unChristian: What A New Generation Really Thinks about Christianity . . . and Why It Matters* (Grand Rapids, MI: Baker Books, 2007), 27.

5. Pew Forum on Religion & Public Life, "In U.S., Decline of Christianity Continues at Rapid Pace," Pew Research Center, October 17, 2019, https://www.pewforum.org/2019/10/17/in-u-s-decline-of-christianity-continues-at-rapid-pace, accessed October 1, 2020.

6. Alan Roxburgh, *Joining God, Remaking Church, Changing the World: The New Shape of the Church in Our Time* (New York: Church Publishing, 2015), 3.

7. J. Kameron Carter covers this topic in *Race: A Theological Account* (Oxford: Oxford University Press, 2008).

8. Margaret Kohn and Kavita Reddy, "Colonialism," in *The Stanford Encyclopedia of Philosophy*, ed. Edward N. Zalta (Fall 2017), https://plato.stanford.edu/archives/fall2017/entries/colonialism, accessed October 10, 2020.

9. "Definition of Colonialism," Lexico, https://www.lexico.com/en/definition/colonialism, accessed October 10, 2020.

10. Eric H. F. Law and Stephanie Spellers, *The Episcopal Way*, Church's Teachings for a Changing World, vol. 1 (New York: Church Publishing, 2014), 21.

11. Law and Spellers, 19.

12. Roxburgh, 11.

13. Tomáš Halík, "Christianity in a Time of Sickness," *America: The Jesuit Review*, April 3, 2020, https://www.americamagazine.org/faith/2020/04/03/christianity-time-sickness, accessed July 26, 2020.

14. *Merriam-Webster*, s.v. "racism," https://www.merriam-webster.com/dictionary/racism, accessed October 12, 2020.

15. Willie James Jennings, "Overcoming Racial Faith: How Christianity Became Entangled with Racism," *Divinity* magazine 14, no. 2 (Spring 2015): 7, https://divinity.duke.edu/sites/divinity.duke.edu/files/divinity-magazine/DukeDivinityMag_Spring15.WEB_.compressed.pdf, accessed November 13, 2020.

16. Roxburgh, 7.

Chapter 2: New Hope for Beloved Community

1. Vida D. Scudder, *The Church and the Hour: Reflections of a Socialist Churchwoman* (New York: Dutton & Co., 1917), 62.
2. Charles Marsh, "The Civil Rights Movement as Theological Drama," in *The Role of Ideas in the Civil Rights South*, ed. Ted Ownby, (Jackson: University Press of Mississippi, 2002), 21.
3. Martin Luther King Jr., "Facing the Challenge of a New Age," speech, December 3, 1956, Martin Luther King Jr. Papers Project, https://kinginstitute.stanford.edu/king-papers/documents/facing-challenge -new-age-address-delivered-first-annual-institute-nonviolence>, accessed October 2, 2020.
4. Howard Thurman, *The Luminous Darkness* (New York: Harper & Row, 1965), 112–13.
5. According to Gary Herstein, King's dissertation bibliography includes Royce's *The Problem of Christianity*. He was also a member of the Fellowship of Reconciliation, the very organization Royce helped to found. See Herstein, "The Roycean Roots of the Beloved Community," *The Pluralist* 4, no. 2 (2009): 91–107.
6. Georg Wilhelm Friedrich Hegel, *Lectures on the Philosophy of Religion*, vol. 3, ed. Peter C. Hodgson (Berkeley: University of California Press, 1985), 372, quoted in Marsh, 8.
7. Josiah Royce, *The Problem of Christianity: The Christian Doctrine of Life* (New York: MacMillan Co., 1913), 196, quoted in Marsh, 8.
8. Royce, xxv.
9. Herstein, 98.
10. House of Bishops Theology Comittee, "White Supremacy, the Beloved Community, and Learning to Listen," 2020 report, 13, https://episcopalchurch.org/files/documents/hob_theo_cmte_report _on_white_supremacy.pdf, accessed September 29, 2020.
11. Verna Dozier, *The Dream of God: A Call to Return* (New York: Seabury Books, 2006), 106.
12. Christopher Duraisingh, "Toward a Postcolonial Re-visioning of the Church's Faith, Witness, and Communion," in *Beyond Colonial Anglicanism: The Anglican Communion in the Twenty-First Century,*

ed. Ian T. Douglas and Kwok Pui-lan (New York: Church Publishing, 2001), 347.
13. Duraisingh, 347.

Chapter 3: The Origins of the Nightmare

1. Isabel Wilkerson, "This History Is Long; This History Is Deep," interview by Krista Tippett, *On Being with Krista Tippett* podcast, June 18, 2020.
2. Henri Nouwen, *You Are the Beloved: Daily Meditations for Spiritual Living* (New York: Convergent Books, 2017), 7.
3. Duraisingh, 344.
4. Roxanne Dunbar-Ortiz, *An Indigenous People's History of the United States* (Boston: Beacon Press, 2015), 32–33.
5. Dunbar-Ortiz, 39.
6. "Dum Diversas," Doctrine of Discovery, https://doctrineofdiscovery .org/dum-diversas, accessed July 29, 2020.
7. Dunbar-Ortiz, 199.
8. The Bull "Romanus Pontifex," Doctrine of Discovery, https://doctrineofdiscovery.org/the-bull-romanus-pontifex-nicholas-v, accessed July 29, 2020.
9. "John Cabot," History.com, https://www.history.com/topics/exploration /john-cabot, accessed August 14, 2020.
10. Jared Diamond, *Guns, Germs and Steel: The Fates of Human Societies* (New York: Norton & Co., 1999).
11. "Requerimiento," Doctrine of Discovery, https://doctrineofdiscovery .org/requerimiento, accessed July 29, 2020.
12. Dunbar-Ortiz, 36.
13. Kelly Brown Douglas, *Stand Your Ground: Black Bodies and the Justice of God* (Maryknoll, NY: Orbis Books, 2015), 3.
14. Douglas, 8.
15. Ben Franklin, "Observations Concerning the Increase of Mankind, Peopling of Countries, etc.," http://www.columbia.edu/~lmg21/ash 3002y/earlyac99/documents/observations.html, accessed August 14, 2020.
16. Thomas Hart Benton, "Speech to Congress, 1846," quoted in Douglas, 32. Original quote can be found in *Congressional Globe* 29, no. 1 (1846): 917–18.

17. James P. Collins, "Native Americans in the Census, 1860–1890," *National Archives Geneaology Notes* 38, no. 2 (Summer 2006), https://www.archives.gov/publications/prologue/2006/summer/indian-census.html, accessed November 15, 2020.

18. "Trail of Tears," History.com, https://www.history.com/topics/native -american-history/trail-of-tears, accessed August 14, 2020.

19. Chief Justice Roger Taney opinion, cited in Martin Magnusson, "No Rights Which the White Man Was Bound to Respect: The Dred Scott Decision," American Constitution Society Expert Forum, https://www.acslaw.org/expertforum/no-rights-which-the-white -man-was-bound-to-respect/, accessed August 16, 2020.

20. W. E. B. Du Bois, *The Suppression of the African Slave-Trade to the United States of America*, vol. 1 (New York: Longmans, Green and Co., 1896), 179.

21. Douglas, 76.

22. "Asian Immigration," Immigration History, https://immigration history.org/lesson-plan/asian-migration, accessed August 19, 2020.

23. Douglas, 26.

24. David Bernstein, "Is It Time for Progressives to Stop Venerating FDR?" *Washington Post*, December 7, 2016, https://www.washington post.com/news/volokh-conspiracy/wp/2016/12/07/is-it-time-for -progressives-to-stop-venerating-fdr/, accessed August 19, 2020.

25. "American Democracy: A Great Leap of Faith" exhibit, Smithsonian National Museum of American History, https://americanhistory .si.edu/democracy-exhibition/vote-voice/keeping-vote/state-rules -federal-rules/literacy-tests, accessed August 19, 2020.

26. Amelia Cheatham, "United States Detention of Child Migrants," Council on Foreign Relations, https://www.cfr.org/backgrounder/us -detention-child-migrants, accessed on August 19, 2020.

27. "Pine Ridge Indian Reservation," https://www.re-member.org/pine -ridge-reservation.aspx, accessed November 15, 2020.

28. Deidre McPhillips, "COVID-19's Tragic Effect on American Indians: A State-by-State Analysis," U.S. News and World Report, October 7, 2020, https://www.usnews.com/news/healthiest-communities/ articles/2020-10-07/a-state-by-state-analysis-of-the-impact-of-covid -19-on-native-americans, accessed November 20, 2020.

29. Michael Gelb, "Native Americans 'Disproportional' Victims of Fatal Police Shootings," The Crime Report, June 30, 2020, https://

thecrimereport.org/2020/06/30/native-americans-disproportional -victims-of-fatal-police-shootings, accessed November 20, 2020.

Chapter 4: The Church of Empire

1. Frederick Douglass, "What to the Slave Is the Fourth of July?" address to the Rochester Ladies' Anti-Slavery Society, July 5, 1852, https://teachingamericanhistory.org/library/document/what-to-the -slave-is-the-fourth-of-july, accessed July 1, 2020.
2. "Elizabethan Settlement," *An Episcopal Dictionary of the Church*, https://episcopalchurch.org/library/glossary/elizabethan-settlement, accessed October 3, 2020.
3. Kwok Pui-Lan, "The Legacy of Cultural Hegemony in the Anglican Church," in *Beyond Colonial Anglicanism*, 47.
4. See liturgies for Morning and Evening Prayer, Prayers and Thanksgivings, and Holy Communion in *The 1662 Book of Common Prayer*, The Church of England, https://www.churchofengland.org/ prayer-and-worship/worship-texts-and-resources/book-common -prayer, accessed January 3, 2021.
5. Dwight Zscheile, *People of the Way: Renewing Episcopal Identity* (New York: Morehouse Publishing, 2012), 20.
6. *The Truth Shall Make You Free: The Lambeth Conference 1988* (London: Church Publishing, 1988), 88.
7. "Religion at Jamestown," Jamestown–Yorktown Foundation, https:// www.historyisfun.org/pdf/background-essays/religionatjamestown .pdf, accessed August 14, 2020.
8. "Religion at Jamestown."
9. Dunbar-Ortiz, 60.
10. Samuel G. Drake, *Biography and History of the Indians of North America* (Boston: 1841), quoted in Dunbar-Ortiz, 60.
11. John Grenier, *The First Way of War: American War Making on the Frontier, 1607–1814* (Cambridge: Cambridge University Press, 2012), 4–5, 7; quoted in Dunbar-Ortiz, 59.
12. Dunbar-Ortiz, 55.
13. "G O: Liverpool Episode," *Traveling the Way of Love* video series, https://episcopalchurch.org/twol/special-episode-go, accessed October 5, 2020.

14. Ariela J. Gross, *What Blood Won't Tell: A History of Race on Trial in America* (Cambridge: Harvard University Press, 2008), quoted in Isabel Wilkerson, *Caste: The Origins of Our Discontents* (New York: Random House, 2020), 45.
15. "Truth and Reconciliation Pilgrimage to Ghana," The Episcopal Church, https://episcopalchurch.org/reconciliation-pilgrimage, accessed October 5, 2020.
16. Harold Lewis, *Yet with a Steady Beat: The African American Struggle for Recognition in the Episcopal Church* (Valley Forge, PA: Trinity Press, 1996), 18.
17. James Gillespie Birney, *The American Churches: The Bulwarks of American Slavery* (Newburyport, MA: Charles Whipple, 1842), 35.
18. Samuel Wilberforce, *A History of the Protestant Episcopal Church in America* (London: Rivingtons, 1856), 429.
19. Walter Posey, "The Protestant Episcopal Church: An American Adaptation," *The Journal of Southern History* 25, no. 1 (February 1959): 26.
20. Elisabeth Evans Wray, "The Relationship of the Protestant Episcopal Church in Virginia with the Negro Slaves 1830–1860: Success or Failure?" (master's thesis, University of Richmond, Virginia, 1977), 6.
21. Wray, 34.
22. The Roberson Project on Slavery, Race, and Reconciliation at the University of the South, "Closer to Home . . ." Facebook, August 5, 2020, https://www.facebook.com/SewaneeProjectonRaceandReconciliation/posts/2776819595918337.
23. Gwynedd Cannan, "Unearthing Our Past," February 14, 2004, https://www.trinitywallstreet.org/blogs/news/unearthing-our-past, accessed November 15, 2020.
24. William Goodell, *Slavery and Anti-Slavery: A History of the Great Struggle in Both Hemispheres* (New York: William Harned Inc., 1852), 194.
25. Gardiner H. Shattuck Jr., *Episcopalians and Race: Civil War to Civil Rights* (Lexington: University of Kentucky Press, 2000), 9.
26. Ronald Levy, "Bishop Hopkins and the Dilemma of Slavery," *The Pennsylvania Magazine of History and Biography* 91, no. 1 (January 1967): 56–71.
27. Levy, 59.

28. "Letter from the Rt. Rev. John H. Hopkins, D.D., LL.D., Bishop of Vermont on the Bible View of Slavery," quoted in Levy, 65.

29. George Freeman, "The Rights and Duties of Slave-Holders," November 1836, http://catalog.hathitrust.org/Record/009562173, accessed January 3, 2021.

30. John Jay II, "The American Church and the African Slave Trade: Speech to the Diocese of New York Convention on September 27, 1860," http://anglicanhistory.org/usa/jjay/convention1860.html, accessed on August 4, 2020.

31. Anna Julia Cooper, *A Voice from the South* (Xenia, OH: Aldine Printing House, 1892) 42.

32. *Journal of the Diocese of Virginia 64th Annual Convention 1859*, 36, quoted in Wray, 66.

33. Renee McKenzie, "Being the Advocate," *Anglican and Episcopal History* 83, no. 2 (June 2014): 167.

34. House of Bishops Theology Committee, 16.

35. Account provided during Equal Justice Initiative Museum Tour, November 18, 2019. www.eji.com.

36. John L. Kater Jr., "Experiment in Freedom: The Episcopal Church and the Black Power Movement," *Historical Magazine of the Protestant Episcopal Church* 48, no. 1 (March 1979): 69.

37. Lewis, 152.

38. House of Bishops Theology Committee, 39.

39. House of Bishops Theology Committee, 40.

40. "Against Inclusivity: Reclaiming Our Ministry as Latinos," Teología en Conjunto conference of Hispanic/Latino Theologians at Episcopal Theological Seminary of the Southwest, 2001, compiled in "Bread for the Journey: An Online Companion to Radical Welcome," 21, https://www.churchpublishing.org/siteassets/pdf/radical-welcome--embracing-god-the-other/wisewords.pdf, accessed January 3, 2021.

41. Posey, 30. See also *Handbook of Religion and Social Institutions*, ed. Helen Rose Ebaugh (New York: Springer, 2006), 191.

42. Pew Forum on Religion & Public Life, "2014 Religious Landscape Study: Episcopalians/Anglicans in the Mainline Tradition," Pew Research Center https://www.pewforum.org/religious-landscape-study/religious-family/episcopaliananglican-family-mainline-trad, accessed November 14, 2020.

43. Kit Konolige and Frederica Konolige, *The Power of Their Glory: America's Ruling Class: The Episcopalians* (New York: Simon & Schuster, 1978), 29.

44. Konolige and Konolige, 29.

Chapter 5: Shards of Light

1. "The Reverend Paul Washington 1921–2002," The Church Awakens: African Americans and the Struggle for Justice exhibit, Episcopal Church Archives, https://episcopalarchives.org/church-awakens/exhibits/show/leadership/clergy/washington, accessed November 15, 2020.

2. "The Episcopal Convention and the Rebellion," *New York Tribune*, October 7, 1861, and *The Church Intelligencer*, October 11, 1861, cited in Robert Trendel, "John Jay II: Antislavery Conscience of the Episcopal Church," *Historical Magazine of the Protestant Episcopal Church* 15, no. 3 (September 1976): 248.

3. Robert A. McCaughey, *Stand Columbia: A History of Columbia University in the City of New York, 1754–2004* (New York: Columbia University Press, 2003), 85, cited in Jared Odessky, "'Possessed of but One Idea Himself': John Jay II's Challenges to Columbia on Slavery and Race," Columbia University and Slavery Project, https://columbiaandslavery.columbia.edu/content/possessed-one-idea-himself-john-jay-iis-challenges-columbia-slavery-and-race #/top, accessed August 27, 2020.

4. John Jay II, "Thoughts on the Duty of the Episcopal Church in Relation to Slavery: Being a Speech Delivered in the New York Anti-Slavery Society Convention" (New York: Pierce and Reed, 1839), 1–11.

5. Odessky.

6. Alexander Crummell, "Jubilate: A Sermon," in *The Shades and the Lights of a Fifty Years' Ministry: 1844–1894* (Washington, DC: St. Luke's Church, 1894), 23, cited in Odessky.

7. "An Episcopalian [John Jay II] to the Editor of the *New York American*," August 26, 1839, in *The Emancipator*, October 3, 1839.

8. Trendel, 244.

9. Odessky.
10. Trendel, 245.
11. Trendel, 246.
12. Eric Foner, *Gateway to Freedom: The Hidden History of the Underground Railroad* (New York: W. W. Norton & Company, 2015), 112, cited in Odessky.
13. "Rector to the Editor," January 17, 1860, *New York Evening Post*, cited in Trendel, 247.
14. Jay, "The American Church and the African Slave Trade."
15. Jay, "The American Church and the African Slave Trade."
16. The Right Reverend Andrew ML Dietsche, "Address to the 243rd Convention of the Episcopal Diocese of New York," November 9, 2019, https://www.dioceseny.org/diocesan-convention-votes-1-1-million-towards-reparations-passes-1860-anti-slavery-resolutions, accessed October 5, 2020.
17. Vida Dutton Scudder, *On Journey* (New York: E. P. Dutton & Co., Inc., 1937), 67, quoted in Douglas M. Strong, *They Walked in the Spirit: Personal Faith and Social Action in America* (Louisville, KY: Westminster John Knox Press, 1997), 66.
18. Scudder, *On Journey*, 84, as quoted in Strong, 67.
19. Vida Dutton Scudder, *My Quest for Reality* (New York: E. P. Dutton, 1952), 93–94, as quoted in Strong, 67.
20. Prayer credited to General William Booth in his final address to the Salvation Army in 1912, https://www.salvationarmy.org/nhqblog/news/2012-05-09-ill-fight-100-years-since-booths-final-address, accessed January 3, 2021.
21. Strong, 67–68.
22. Strong, 70.
23. Scudder, *The Church and the Hour*, 36, 51.
24. Scudder, *On Journey*, 384.
25. Gibson Winter, *The Suburban Captivity of the Churches: An Analysis of Protestant Responsibility in the Expanding Metropolis* (New York: MacMillan Co., 1962).
26. Shattuck, 133–34.
27. Wade H. Morris, "Contrary to the Mind and Will of God: White Flight and the Desegregation of Southern Episcopal Schools," *American Educational History Journal*, 46, no. 2 (2019): 21–24.

28. Shattuck, 112.
29. "Jonathan Daniels 1939–1965," The Church Awakens: African Americans and the Struggle for Justice exhibit, Episcopal Church Archives, https://episcopalarchives.org/church-awakens/exhibits/show/escru/jonathan-daniels, accessed August 27, 2020.
30. Jonathan Daniels, "Eulogy (a Reflection on Participation in Civil Rights Movement)," The Church Awakens exhibit, https://episcopalarchives.org/church-awakens/items/show/166, accessed August 27, 2020.
31. Jonathan Daniels, "But My Heart is Black," *The Texas Observer*, October 29, 1965 (published posthumously).
32. Daniels, "But My Heart is Black."
33. "Jonathan Daniels," The Church Awakens.
34. "Jonathan Daniels," The Church Awakens.
35. "Jonathan Daniels," The Church Awakens.
36. "Washington," The Church Awakens.
37. Paul Washington with David Mcl. Gracie, *"Other Sheep I Have": The Autobiography of Father Paul M. Washington* (Philadelphia: Temple University Press, 1994), 7.
38. McKenzie, 167.
39. Washington, 25.
40. Washington, 26.
41. Washington, 56.
42. Washington, 42.
43. Washington, 148.
44. Washington, 171.
45. Washington, 161.
46. William R. Macklin and Mark Wagenveld, "The Rev. Paul Washington, Voice of the Oppressed, Dies," *Philadelphia Inquirer*, October 9, 2002.

Chapter 6: Lose Your Life—Kenosis

1. Matthew 10:39.
2. Roxburgh, 51.
3. Cynthia Bourgeault, "Insights at the Edge: Encountering the Wisdom Jesus," *Sounds True* podcast, June 21, 2011, https://www.resources.soundstrue.com/podcast/cynthia-bourgealt-encountering-the-wisdom-jesus.

4. Andrew Root, *Faith Formation in a Secular Age* (Grand Rapids, MI: Baker Academic, 2017), 162.

5. Root, 163.

6. Pema Chödrön, *Practicing Peace* (Boulder, CO: Shambhala, 2006), https://www.shambhala.com/not-biting-the-hook-an-excerpt-from -practicing-peace, accessed September 1, 2020.

7. Chödrön.

8. Bourgeault.

9. Paolo Freire, *Pedagogy of the Oppressed* (Maryknoll, NY: Orbis Books, 1970), 109.

10. Tammerie Day, *Constructing Solidarity for a Liberative Ethic: Anti-Racism, Action, and Justice* (New York: Palgrave Macmillan, 2012), 107.

11. H. A. Goodman, "The Real Reasons Many White People Can't Empathize with Ferguson, Racial Disparities, or Black Suffering," *Huffington Post*, August 27, 2014, https://www.huffpost.com/entry/ the-real-reasons-many-whi_b_5721248.

12. Goodman.

13. Sam Osherson, PhD, "White Sorrow and a Positive Racial Identity," *Psychology Today*, September 8, 2019, https://www.psychology today.com/us/blog/listen/201909/white-sorrow-and-positive-racial -identity, accessed September 1, 2020.

14. Osherson, "White Sorrow."

15. Day, 113.

16. See Janet Helms, *A Race Is a Nice Thing to Have: A Guide to Being a White Person or Understanding the White Persons in Your Life* (San Diego: Cognella, 2020). Also see "An Update of Helms's White and People of Color Racial Identity Models," in *Handbook of Multicultural Counseling*, ed. J. G. Ponterotto, J. M. Casas, L. A. Suzuki, and C. M. Alexander (Thousand Oaks, CA: Sage, 1995), 181–191.

17. Racial Equity Tools, "Developing a Positive White Identity," https:// www.racialequitytools.org/resourcefiles/positive_white_identity.pdf, accessed November 16, 2020.

18. Day, 115. Adapted by author.

19. Day, 117.

Chapter 7: Gain Your Life—Solidarity

1. Scudder, *The Church and the Hour*, 74.
2. Daniels, "But My Heart is Black."
3. Gustavo Gutiérrez, *A Theology of Liberation: History, Politics, and Salvation*, 15th anniv. ed. (Maryknoll, NY: Orbis Books, 1988), 118.
4. Ada María Isasi-Díaz, "Solidarity: Love of Neighbor in the 21st Century," in *Lift Every Voice: Constructing Christian Theologies from the Underside*, ed. Susan Brooks Thistlethwaite and Mary Potter Engel (Maryknoll, NY: Orbis Books, 1998), 32.
5. Douglas, 171.
6. Duraisingh, 353.
7. Kelly M. Hoffman, Sophie Trawalter, Jordan R. Axt, and M. Norman Oliver, "Racial Bias in Pain Assessment and Treatment Recommendations, and False Beliefs about Biological Differences between Blacks and Whites," *Proceedings of the National Academy of Sciences of the United States of America* 113, no. 16 (April 19, 2016): 4296–4301, https://www.pnas.org/content/113/16/4296, accessed November 16, 2020.
8. Matteo Forgiarini, Marcello Gallucci, and Angelo Maravita, "Racism and the Empathy for Pain on Our Skin," *Frontiers in Psychology* 2, no. 108 (May 23, 2011), https://www.frontiersin.org/articles/10.3389 /fpsyg.2011.00108/full, accessed November 16, 2020.
9. I owe credit for this phrase to the Reverend Kerlin Richter. Years ago, she was helping me to plan a workshop for a diocese that was anxious about terms like "anti-racism." She said, "I think what you're really talking about is stewardship of privilege. I can't simply drop all my privilege, but I can use it for the cause."

Chapter 8: Walk in Love—Discipleship

1. David Swanson, *Rediscipling the White Church: From Cheap Diversity to True Solidarity* (Downers Grove, Illinois: InterVarsity Press, 2020), 1.

2. "The Way of Love," the Episcopal Church, https://episcopalchurch
.org/jesus-shaped-lifeanglican-discipleship.

3. Scudder, *On Journey*, 384.

4. Oliver, "Against Inclusivity: Reclaiming Our Ministry as Latinos,"
23.

Conclusion: God Bless the Cracks

1. Douglass, "What to the Slave Is the Fourth of July?"

ABOUT EDUCATION FOR MINISTRY

Do you have questions about your faith? Most people do, and most find it challenging to get answers. Education for Ministry (EfM) was developed by the School of Theology in Sewanee, Tennessee, to provide a mechanism for people to work through those questions. This four-year course of study is led by a mentor who provides the framework for the group to connect faith to their daily lives through reading and discussion.

Meeting once a week in small groups with people from your neighborhood, you will begin to think theologically, reflect faithfully, and speak civilly when confronted by beliefs and principles in opposition to your own. And that's something we can all appreciate in today's world.

By being an EfM participant, you will learn how to articulate your faith. You will learn how to shape your faith into action. You will become involved in ministries in your community, and you will make a difference.

Since the inception of this vital program in 1976, more than 95,000 people have participated in it. EfM groups meet regionally in nearly every diocese of The Episcopal Church, in six provinces of the Anglican Communion, and in virtual classrooms with participants from across the globe. We would love to have you join us!

For complete details, visit efm.sewanee.edu.

CPSIA information can be obtained
at www.ICGtesting.com
Printed in the USA
JSHW022351190122
22113JS00009B/344